The Political Status
of Puerto Rico

The Political Status
of Puerto Rico

Edited by
Pamela S. Falk
Columbia University

Foreword by
Luis Rafael Sánchez

An Americas Society Book

Lexington Books
D.C. Heath and Company/Lexington, Massachusetts/Toronto

Library of Congress Cataloging-in-Publication Data

The Political status of Puerto Rico.

  Bibliography: p.
  Includes index.
  1. Puerto Rico—Politics and government—1952–
2. Puerto Rico—Economic conditions—1952–
3. Puerto Rico—Foreign relations—United States.
4. United States—Foreign relations—Puerto Rico.
I. Falk, Pamela S.
F1976.P58   1986   327.7295073   84–47504
ISBN 0–669–08279–1 (alk. paper)

Published simultaneously in Canada
Printed in the United States of America
Casebound International Standard Book Number: 0–669–08279–1
Library of Congress Catalog Card Number: 84–47504

The paper used in this publication meets the minimum requirements of American National Standard for Information Sciences—Permanence of Paper for Printed Library Materials, ANSI Z39.48–1984.
⊗™

The last numbers on the right below indicate the number and date of printing.

10 9 8 7 6 5 4 3 2 1

95 94 93 92 91 90 89 88 87 86

Contents

Part II Political Leaders Speak 23

Part III Economic Issues 39

Part IV International Implications 53

Letter from the Americas Society President

Ambassador George W. Landau

T he Americas Society is a nonprofit, private institution established in 1981 to coordinate the activities of various U.S. organizations dealing with hemispheric affairs, including Mexico, Central and South America, the Caribbean, and Canada. The Society, which is national in scope, is located in New York City, with affiliates in New York, Washington, and Miami, including the Center for Inter-American Relations, the Council of the Americas, the Pan American Society of the United States, and Caribbean/Central American Action.

Among the objectives of the Americas Society is to provide a forum for the discussion of issues vital to the hemisphere and to improve understanding of the economic, political, and cultural values of all countries of the Americas. The Americas Society seeks to provide a forum through which leaders from government, business, academia, the media, the arts, politics, and other areas can make their thoughts known to diverse national and international audiences.

The purpose of this book—to discuss the status of Puerto Rico from a political, economic, and international perspective, as well as from the viewpoint of United States–Puerto Rico relations—clearly falls within the agenda of activities undertaken by the Americas Society. Through its publication, we hope to expand our efforts by reaching those who are interested in this subject but are not able to participate personally in our activities. Along with previous and forthcoming volumes sponsored by the Americas Society and its affiliates, it is hoped that this book will contribute significantly to the permanent body of research and commentary on this and related subjects.

Preface
Public Information and the Political
Status of Puerto Rico

Russell E. Marks, Jr.
Senior Vice-President, Haley Associates, and
Former President, Americas Society

I n May 1982, the Center for Inter-American Relations, an affiliate of the Americas Society, initiated a project entitled "Public Information and the Political Status of Puerto Rico," which is completed with publication of this book. The primary goal of the project was to improve national understanding of the political status debate in Puerto Rico. The subsidiary objective was to analyze previous press coverage of the Puerto Rican political experience in general and the status debate in particular.

The project, generously supported by the Ford Foundation and the Angel Ramos Foundation of San Juan, was structured to allow analysis of the Puerto Rican political experience from the differing viewpoints of politicians, scholars, and business people, first in a public seminar and then in this anthology. As the first part of the project, the Center for Inter-American Relations sponsored a three-day conference in March 1983. Representatives of print and broadcast news organizations—including the *Wall Street Journal,* the *New York Times, Newsweek, Time* magazine, *El Diario,* the UPI and AP wire services, *Noticias del Mundo, El Nuevo Dia,* the *New York Daily News,* the *Village Voice,* WOR-TV, CBS "Special Events" and "60 Minutes," PBS "Frontline" and "Inside Story," Channel 41, and SIN, among others—attended the conference in addition to business executives, academics, and government officials.

This book, based on the work of conference participants, also includes material by experts who were unable to attend the conference as commentary by the heads of all three political parties in Puerto Rico, representing the status options. We believe it provides an authoritative account of the political status debate in its historical context.

The Americas Society/Center for Inter-American Relations is pleased to provide this reference work to facilitate broader understanding of the issues that still trouble the island–continental relationship.

Introduction

Pamela S. Falk
Director, Puerto Rico Project, Americas Society
Associate Director, Institute of Latin American and
Iberian Studies, Columbia University

F
ew mainland Americans are aware that the overwhelming majority of
Puerto Rico's 3.25 million citizens favor changes in the island's present political arrangement with the United States. Whether statehood,
a modified form of commonwealth, or full independence would best meet
Puerto Rico's needs remains a question of heated debate. The United States
cannot remain aloof from this decision-making process, because the desirability of a status change necessarily depends on Washington's policies toward
Puerto Rico.

Contradictions abound in Puerto Rico's present status. How can it be
that a citizen of the United States, as every Puerto Rican resident is, cannot
vote for the president of the United States? Yet, by moving to the mainland—
which any Puerto Rican has the unfettered legal right to do—that same
individual may vote for president. Why is a male Puerto Rican required to
register for the draft of the U.S. Army? And if Puerto Rican residents may
not vote for president, isn't it hard to understand why they may vote in the
Republican and Democratic party primaries for the selection of a presidential
candidate for whom they cannot vote in the general election?

The economic dilemmas that face Puerto Rico are equally compelling.
Over 62 percent of Puerto Ricans on the island live below the national
poverty level, the 1980 U.S. Census reported, while U.S. subsidies to the
Puerto Rican economy in the form of food stamps and other programs are
estimated at $10 billion annually. Moreover, U.S. corporations may make
"tax-exempt" investments under a 1921 federal tax provision, but on a per
capita basis, according to the Puerto Rican Economic Development Association, Puerto Rico receives only half the federal assistance that the fifty U.S.
states receive. Contradictions abound.

Despite islanders' interest in a status change, only one plebiscite has been
held—in 1967. The largest party in Puerto Rico, the New Progressive Party
(PNP) advocates statehood. The Party's principal spokesman, former Governor Carlos Romero Barceló, who was first elected in 1976 and lost his bid
for a third term in 1984, indefinitely postponed the referendum on statehood
when his predicted 1980 landslide failed to materialize.

Public discussion and study has focused on the pros and cons of statehood. Supporters of this option point to Puerto Rico's gradual integration into the economic and political life of the United States. They argue that a shift to Puerto Rican statehood would be the logical course to continue the island's political and economic development. Full representation in Congress, according to the statehooders, would reflect Puerto Rico's political responsibility and importance to the United States, and accordingly, the new state would gain greater influence over issues affecting the island.

PNP

Even fervent supporters of statehood admit, however, that many obstacles lie ahead. Congress might feel compelled to impose English as Puerto Rico's official language. The economic consequences of statehood might be disadvantageous: the government of Puerto Rico could lose the federal rebates on duties and excise taxes it now receives; under present federal law, three of the island's largest banks would be forced to cease operating; and federal income taxes would be imposed for the first time. Supporters of statehood argue, however, that most economic difficulties resulting from a status change could be avoided if Puerto Rico were accorded both special transitional assistance and a 20-year phase-in period for federal taxes and regulations.

By contrast, the advocates of a modified commonwealth—the Popular Democratic Party (the party of the present governor), which had electoral support approximately equal to the PNP in 1980—favor a political status similar to the current association with the United States, but with increased benefits.

PPD

Most supporters of a modified commonwealth believe that the island's "free association" with the United States has been advantageous; it avoids complete assimilation into the United States and gives relative autonomy. Advocates of the modified status option are generally satisfied with the current economic arrangements. They believe that the low minimum wage and the present corporate tax exemption program are needed to maintain the island's growth. They argue that commonwealth status alone should not bar Puerto Rico from federal assistance in block grants.

PIP

The Puerto Rican Independence Party (PIP)—led by a member of the Puerto Rican Senate, Rubén Berríos Martínez—is the most influential of the two independence parties and is the only registered party that advocates independence. The Puerto Rican Socialist Party (PSP), lost its registration as a local political party. Independence advocates have argued to the Decolonization Committee of the United Nations that Puerto Rico is entitled to self-determination and that as an independent nation, Puerto Rico would be able to establish its own foreign economic and political policies and would be able to apply to the United States for foreign assistance, which is unavailable now.

Independentistas concede that the large federal subsidy programs would be eliminated and that the government of Puerto Rico would have to assume many of the federal government's responsibilities regarding the economy, defense, and foreign affairs. The PIP's proposal to maintain a policy of non-alignment includes the elimination of the U.S. military presence in Puerto Rico and the establishment of a development strategy that would emphasize agricultural development and full employment and would attempt to decrease the island's economic dependence on the United States.

Advocates of all three status positions agree that the U.S. Congress, and therefore the mainland residents, have significant political and economic power over the island's destiny.

This book presents the Puerto Rican political status debate in its full dimension. Puerto Rican political leaders and policy experts, mainland policymakers, and business leaders all have their say. The Americas Society Puerto Rico Project, described in the Preface, investigated the status debate in three unique ways. First, it brought Puerto Rico's political leaders to New York to describe the status option that each party advocates. Second, it educated the mainland media—both print and broadcast—about the significance of Puerto Rico as a U.S. national issue. Finally, this book was prepared to provide the American public, in Puerto Rico and on the mainland, with the necessary background on the economics and politics—on the local, national, and international levels—involved in the political status debate.

In the foreword, "Don't Cry for Us, Puerto Rico," Luis Rafael Sánchez, Puerto Rican essayist and playwright, states: "The country of Puerto Rico, tempestuous in its confusion, assaulted by self-devouring violence—pathetic violence without promise—divided into three hostile denouements, Puerto Rico is a country that pushes its way toward sorrow." He concludes: "Puerto Rico is the bitter country that we have made or have allowed to be made bitter for us."

In a dreamlike description of San Juan's Fourth of July celebration—so symbolically important to the relationship between the island and the mainland—Luis Rafael Sánchez weaves a tale, in a style that has been described as "neon prose," of local *jíbaros* and city dwellers, depicting the cultural impact of the overlap of the two cultures and histories.

The opinions in the various articles presented here differ—particularly in their interpretation of the ties between San Juan and Washington—but Luis Rafael Sánchez's foreword introduces the anthology with a very common theme: Changes must be made in the island's status to rectify an imbalance. Later in the book, Miami's former mayor, Maurice Ferre calls this imbalance the "unfulfilled" side of "Puerto Rican dignity"; Governor Rafael Hernández Colón argues, "This is not the Puerto Rico that we want, but it is the only one we have and love"; and San Juan's Mayor Baltasar Corrada del Río states, "Although the world has been reshaped, reconstructed and rebuilt more than once in our time, the island remains stagnant with a political status of ambiguity and indecision." Puerto Rican politics, New York Congressman Robert Garcia concludes, "is not an avocation; it is a passion."

Part I of the book, "Background of the Debate," begins with a history of Puerto Rico's independence and a legislative history of the island's association with the United States by Jeffrey Puryear. His thesis departs from the traditional mainland argument that the resolution to the endless debate rests with the Puerto Rican people—a theme sounded by almost all national politicians in the past. Because Washington holds most of the power, "it has the responsibility for setting in motion fundamental changes," he argues. The heart of the issue is not in a new plebiscite but, rather, in first asking national policymakers to decide what they would do if, in fact, the Puerto Rican population decided on a change in status.

The background section includes articles by San Juan's Mayor Baltasar Corrada del Río, who analyzes the current state of disquiet over the status debate from the point of view of a statehood advocate, and Puerto Rico's governor, the Honorable Rafael Hernández Colón, a proponent of a modified Commonwealth, who describes the current political and economic state of the commonwealth.

Part II, "Political Leaders Speak," presents the three major party positions on political status—direct from party leaders: on commonwealth, Senator Miguel A. Hernández Agosto, Popular Democratic Party; on statehood, former Governor Carlos Romero Barceló, New Progressive Party; and on independence, Senator Rubén Berríos Martínez, Puerto Rican Independence Party. Parts III and IV discuss economic issues and international implications, and parts V and VI analyze the overlaps of local and national economic and political issues, respectively. Most important, several contributors specifically address the ambiguities that surround mainland press coverage of Puerto Rico. Both *San Juan Star* columnist Juan Manuel García Passalacqua and George McDougall, former press aide to former Governor Romero Barceló, conclude that Puerto Rico often falls in the cracks of national news coverage and Latin American headlines.

Appendix A sets forth the major legislation that has shaped the relationship between the island and the mainland: the Treaty of Paris between Spain and the United States, which gave Puerto Rico to the United States; the Foraker Act of 1900, which incorporated Puerto Rico as a U.S. territory; the Jones Act of 1917, which gave Puerto Rican residents U.S. citizenship; the 1950 public law that gave Puerto Rico the right to draft its own constitution; and the 1952 public law that gave Puerto Rico its current commonwealth status. Appendix B provides a breakdown of Puerto Rico's election results from 1952 to 1984. Finally, a select bibliography is provided for further analysis.

In the coming years, the mainland–Puerto Rico relationship will be tested by U.S. budget cutbacks, Puerto Rican socioeconomic problems, and increasing support for a status change. Given the clear indigenous mandate for change in Puerto Rico's status and the relative ignorance of most Americans about the plight of the island, the United States–Puerto Rico debate is bound to generate considerable heat. This book is offered in the hope that it will shed some light on the controversy.

Foreword
Don't Cry for Us, Puerto Rico

Luis Rafael Sánchez
(translated by Edith Grossman)

T he posters that invite participation in the Fourth of July parade in San Juan contain a secret discourse that transcends the public discourse by the Governor of Puerto Rico to commemorate this outstanding anniversary, a discourse that is even bolder than the capering of countless baton twirlers, the allegory of the floats, and the exoticism of the dances—they were Arabic last time—performed by a typical Puerto Rican ballet company that, curiously enough, is separated from its devotion to what is typically Puerto Rican by the Fourth of July.

Animated by marching bands whose irrepressible Antilleanism charangas Chopin's "Polonaise," boleroizes "Tales from the Vienna Woods," and salsafies any aria by Puccini—Musetta's outburst in the Café Momus is a standard piece in the repertoire—the baton twirlers, the floats, the exotic dances make their appearance on the Fourth of July to highlight, with civic spirit volatilized by tulle and crepe paper, the public discourse by the Governor of Puerto Rico and to provide the setting of execrable taste that restores the provincial air that suits the country so well: Metropolitan San Juan is the soma of a sickly adolescent or a parish between Barrio Obrero and La Quince. The truth is that it's only a step from Barrio Obrero to any corner, any mountain, any shore in Puerto Rico; its fortune and its misfortune is that the entire country can fit into one hand.

The View from the Camera's Viewfinder

Some snapshots in focused polychrome, chosen from a panorama that highlights enigma and suggestion, confirm the excesses of a subordination that makes even credulity blink at the absurdity that maximizes and exhibits the national symbols of the United States of North America and minimizes and inhibits the national symbols of Puerto Rico.

Let us study this sequence that the viewfinder on an intrepid camera recapitulates and repeats loyally, symptomatically, annually: hundreds of

Puerto Ricans attending the Fourth of July parade in San Juan guerrillafy their desire and carry the North American flag on their shoulders as if it were a rifle, dozens of Puerto Ricans attending the Fourth of July parade in San Juan are protected from the burning sun by broadbrimmed straw hats decorated with little North American flags, dozens of Puerto Ricans attending the Fourth of July parade in San Juan theatricalize their clothing with the allusive red, white, and blue and the crowning multi-starred touch: berets, hairnets, turbans, Panama hats, haircurlers, ribbons to braid your hair. A single idea lies at the heart of this sequence: for hundreds of Puerto Ricans the North American flag is the road to salvation, the ticket to ecstasy, an awesome instrument, the emblem of a religion that guarantees glory on earth.

Irony is produced in the snapshot, one that is not produced during the Fourth of July parade in San Juan. The baroque extravagance of absence: the proud arm that raises the Puerto Rican flag is nowhere to be seen; during the Fourth of July parade in San Juan the Puerto Rican flag is the ignored flag, the closet flag denied by the closet Puerto Rican. (What an impressive comic strip the figure of the closet Puerto Rican would make. How opportune this cataloguing of his vices and evasions.)

On to the Public Discourse

Instead of an analysis ennobled by the moderating tone and measure of its prose—an exemplary, unitary prose that, one supposes, derives its power from the will to democracy—instead of a serene reflection on an exceptional event—a country that achieves sovereignty, takes on its memory and its future and confronts the vehement questioning of the present—an event that the United States of North America commemorates every Fourth of July with a legitimate display of pride, confidence, and nationalism—the government of Puerto Rico is a tired old psalm to the hurricane of kindnesses with which the United States of North America flaunts, pampers, and spoils the Puerto Rican nation, a propagandistic psalm to a servile and uncritical North Americanism, so vulgar that it would make any sensitive, honest North American blush, a myopic psalm that decrees the infinite good fortune enjoyed by the Beloved Territory Across the Sea and the Beloved Metropolis. Lovers, or whatever you call them, lovers who are bedazzled by an irresistible and shameless passion that is rumored to starve and wither both of them—his pocket, her heart; lovers better known by their lyrical epithets "The Colossus of the North" and "The Little Antillean Island."

As if an abundance of froth could substitute for critical imagination and obviate the hunger for critical imagination felt by a country that is characterized by its long-debated agreement with the North American nation and by the forms of its poverty, its geographical and spiritual place within the

Latin American community, the exodus of half of its people to the percussive utopia of the *Big City*—those who suffer and struggle in Spanish are "spiks," those who suffer and struggle in English are "Neorricans"—two different terms for the same contempt.

A Third World Love Story

Yes, the analogy continues (begging Erich Segal's pardon): in the Hollywood manner of a neurasthenic *Love Story* in which The Colossus of the North plays trillionaire Oliver, generous and blond, and The Little Antillean Island plays dark little Jennifer Cavalieri, talkative, poor, but trying hard to cope. A neurasthenic *Love Story,* I called it.

Although year after year more and more of the governed debate the disquiet that such exaggerated love can lead to. Although year after year more and more of the governed suffer the disease that so much well-being entails. Although year after year disenchantment flourishes, multiplies, comes to light, clamors for the moral and legal revision of a political love affair that from its very beginning in 1898 was dominated by the unilateral and arbitrary rule of The Colossus of the North and the inconsequential and powerless voice of The Little Antillean Island, the unilateral and arbitrary rule that feigned cessation and transfer in 1952 with the proclamation of the Associated Free State of Puerto Rico, a deceptive, pompous name in Spanish, a sober, conservative name in English; the baptizers were astute, their bilingualism devious, their diligence cautious.

George Orwell's Mirrors

"Let's face it" means let's forget about mindless sublimities. Let's face it, then: "Commonwealth" is less incoherent than "Associated Free State," less insidious in purpose, less shoddy in morphology, less conflictive in meaning when it imperiously makes the rounds of the cocktail parties at liberal North American universities or at the gala buffets of gringo radical chic—thanks, Tom Wolfe, I also enjoyed *The electric kool-aid acid test.* It is an ambiguous agreement, this Associated Free State—vulnerable, rustic, an agreement that reinvented colonialism, toned down its oppressive colors, altered its nuances, proclaimed its absolute beauty—a beauty that is impossible because it is absolute; it is an agreement that would irritate common sense and good judgment less if it would admit that its colonial defects are its paradoxical virtues, its motive for action, its reason for survival, its safe conduct through the steps toward reasonable modernization that Puerto Rican life is currently taking; it is an agreement that could gain recognition of its controversial singularity if the rhetoric that supports it would resist the temptation to announce a full island autonomy never seen in practice or foreseen or existent on paper, if it would exorcize the fetishism of the United States of North America and Puerto Rico as "equal partners." But if the fetishism is not negotiable, if its exorcism would disturb the slumber of those who rest in the shade of that flowering hope, then the fetishism should contain the fulminating clarification that "Some partners are more equal than others."

"Is Mister David Lean available to shoot the film of this saucy epic?"—this neurasthenic, Wagnerian, Third World *Love Story* whose orchestra has agreed to the vocalizations of a stunning asstress in recognition of the Hamletian whims that tend to be the essence of Puerto Rican politics. *Pay attention please:* the stunning asstress' dress must have a bevy of flounces so that she has plenty of business for her backside. *More attention please:* the stunning asstress must boast a nose that would command the greatest disrespect in Alabama, a most mulattoish Puerto Rican nose that honors and pleases some because it recalls the diverse racial mixtures on which Puerto Rican history is based, and that traumatizes and shames others who hurry to the operating rooms of plastic surgeons: a big spread-nosed mulatta who gives the lie to so many fraudulent lily-white purisms—*freudulent* lily-white purisms.

Decline, Disgust

It is Ionescoean—the nonsensical postulate, if nonsense is really one of the possibilities of knowledge; the end preceded the beginning, second came before first. The postulate stands arithmetic on its head, invalidates logic, and imitates a chapter from *Alice in Wonderland,* the one about the rebellious numbers, "The Queen's Croquet Game." Better yet, that unhinging scene from "The Bald Soprano" in which the Smiths turn their family relationships into chaos and the absurd is imposed as the norm. No doubt about it, the postulate is Ionescoean: to the apoplectic stupefaction of the Democratic Popular Party—which never wanted to or never could point the way to the growth of the Associated Free State—the end precedes the beginning, second comes before first. In 1968 a party assumed political power that was incredulous of the defeated party's miracles and tales of miracles, incredulous of the transaction that the defeated party had organized, administered, and praised, blindly, monographically, since 1952.

Innovation, Progress, Other Calamities

The change from one ruling party to another was achieved with a historic serenity that confirmed and recorded the civic responsibility that the country of Puerto Rico includes in any list of its most valued accomplishments, a responsibility rooted deep in its real contempt for regimes, petrified by terror, that communicate their truths from behind barbed wire, for the coups that divert and enrich a rapacious military—"Show me a poor Latin American colonel and I will show you the fast lane to the moon" are the impassive words to a tango or a stunning Gaucho malambo or a rhythm with Antillean maracas or a chilling samba or a sinister Andean Waltz or a deadly Central American rock and roll tune.

The change occurred, but not innovation or progress. And it gave priority to its outstanding, obsessive, terminal mania: to annex the country of Puerto Rico to the North American nation, to annex the country of Puerto Rico to the North American nation, to annex the country of Puerto Rico to the North American nation—an intransigent incursion into the Kafkaesque suggestions of a broken record.

This Way to the Final Solution, Ladies and Gentlemen

As if the universe were a celluloid, unreal ship by Fellini that would avoid the coasts of Puerto Rico. As if the universe would not be completed with the Puerto Rican manner and custom of bewitching reality. As if the universe would not be diminished by our absence. Naturally it sees as healthy and justified the Yankeefication of Puerto Rico, pressuring it with a birth certificate dated July 25, 1898, bickering over its long life as a nation unfortunately established between the excesses and supervision of metropolises; the Puerto Rican nation, made from scraps, against the tide, among denials, rejections, persecutions, but made, creator of its own social morality, in possession of a differentiated view that is not transferable to the rest of the world, the rest of the universe that grow larger on its smallness.

On to the Secret Discourse

Is it the semiotics of underdevelopment or the underdevelopment of semiotics? The graphic dialectic of joy, fiesta, binges until you're sick of them and other extravagant refinements, the persistent invitation to a drunken spree where lucidity drowns, the downpour of drawings in which complicity is entangled and art is distracted—everything attempts to extenuate the extravagant lie that Puerto Rico is celebrating her independence because the United States of North America is celebrating hers. Or, what is most definitely the same thing, that Puerto Rico does not have to achieve sovereignty because the United States of North America achieved hers two hundred years ago. Nice lie! would be the rhyme of whoever launched it as a trial balloon to see if the henhouse would panic or docilely tolerate still another distortion. Carlos Fuentes insists that everything in Mexico is an insult, and he aims his attack at both the interior and the exterior of the insult in order to denounce and combat it. An approximate paraphrase, an approximate hypothesis: in Puerto Rico everything is a distortion.

When the Northern Lights Are Local

Of course, distortion is a secret sign of incompetence or bad faith. And the sentence *"Come celebrate our nation's independence with us"* is, despite the rejoicing in the Christmasy comics, a kind of revulsive grimace that both experience, and the experience is despair heightened by the difficulties, the bitterness, the anxiety that are the consequences of distortion. The supply of distortion is varied and totally absorbing. But an example chosen at random demonstrates its worst extremes. Puerto Rican news media classify their material under the obvious headings local, national, and international. What is not obvious is the distorted handling of the classifications, the assault on geography, the resolute imposition of demagogic alibis. In the Puerto Rican news media, international means the news that Brigitte Bardot defends the right of seals to a life free of hunters, that Prime Minister Zhao Ziyang drinks Coca Cola, that Octavio Paz has an opinion. Similarly, any news from the United States should also be classified as international.

But distortion comes into play, and distortion means that in the Puerto Rican news media what happens in Washington, San Francisco, or Texas is classified as national. Distortion overflows the limits of incompetence and bad faith when it reduces to merely local, classifies as merely local, the news from Puerto Rico even when it has the indubitable character of a real event: data derived from the aurora borealis by the Astronomical Observatory at Arecibo, the opening concert of the Casals Festival under the outstanding direction of Herbert von Karajan, the return to his native land of José Feliciano. The purpose is inescapable: the effort to make benign and to place above all suspicion the deception that the United States of North America is the nation of the Puerto Ricans, the effort to make people believe that *citizenship and nationality are interchangeable,* the effort to make people believe that Puerto Rico is only a locality in the patio of the United States of North America—a rowdy piece of Antillean property that belongs to the United States of North America, "a beach resort where the best piña coladas can be tasted within the boundaries of the United States of America."

The National Sweat of La Chacón, Georgie Torres, and El Niño de las Monjas

But, sooner or later, the colony hallucinates and the slip-up occurs: the same news media that foment distortion and reduce everything that is Puerto Rican to a merely local presence, classify as *national monuments* the golden fists of Wilfredo Gómez or El Niño de las Monjas, urge the permanent participation of the spectacular Georgie Torres in the *National Basketball Invitational,* and pamper the singer and dancer Iris Chacón with the title of *national super star.*

Suddenly, Last Summer

A word to the wise. I don't repeat myself just for fun, I don't succumb to stylistic demands; it is simply worth repeating: the posters that invite participation in the Fourth of July parade in San Juan contain a secret discourse that transcends the public discourse by the Governor of Puerto Rico to commemorate this outstanding anniversary.

Yes, a slow and subtle reading of a text that demands our attention, *"Come celebrate our nation's independence with us,"* is the result of a certain carelessness in the ideological coordination of the secret discourse, a space the author did not notice through which an unexpected demand is filtered: the nation is a necessity that presses sooner or later. And that necessity, pejoratively reduced by some to mere idea or abstract digression, by others to a refrain by poets who favor romanticuckoo similicadence, or the droolings of telluric villagers, that necessity is accentuated when those who fed on underestimating it, those who undervalued the courage and rigor it invokes—a courage and a rigor at odds with the bel canto flutings to which some reduce the examination of patriotic matters—finally return to it, these cultivators of a hysterical Puertorricanism that is the refuge and subterfuge of improvisors, of careless men and other dabblers in booming oratory that can hardly put out the glow.

Maybe the Dinosaurs

I know, the nation that is venerated in the posters that invite participation in the Fourth of July parade in San Juan is the North American nation. Another thing entirely would be the sequence of a film in the current fact-fiction fad, the adventures of a medium in the next century, the literature of anticipation. Or what is definitely the same thing, the deciphering of the navigation charts of the Congress of the United States of North America through the jurisdictional waters of Puerto Rico: what will it concede and what will it not cede when it's a question of "dear" Puerto Rico?

Irrelevant writing? The topic lost in digression? Trust me: Puerto Rico is the contemporary colony that provokes the most conjectures, that commissions the most heated investigations of its legitimacy, that preserves the most scholarship and compiles the most forensic confrontations. Perhaps the finicky vegetarianism of the dinosaurs provokes more digressions, I don't know. I do know that the "ugly island full of tropical diseases," as Stephen Sondheim so rudely called it, demands a plethora of perspicacity and sobriety from the person who explains or interprets it—an arduous plethora for the person who is born and survives in the hurricane eye of passion (let no one accuse me of objectivity). I know, we all know, that when we use up the arguments and refutations in the case of Puerto Rico, the problem of Puerto Rico, the crossroads of Puerto Rico, the dead end of Puerto Rico, the struggle of Puerto Rico, we will rush in relief to the aid of literature so that it can be a concretion that synthesizes so much complexity and particularity.

Burundunga, Catch 22, Macondo, the kingdoms where obfuscating fevers are denied and where discernment is on perpetual vacation, are synonyms for Puerto Rico. *Catch 22,* my boys: the nation is a necessity that presses sooner or later. Despite the elipsis of the patronymic, despite the fact that the Fourth of July is not a parenthesis that leaves any room for doubt, the predictable carelessness of the secret discourse stresses the fact that the concept of the nation liberates the instinct for ownership. And that the instinct for ownership is not improvised, not adjudicated by an ideocratic caucus or by a specialist in the collective unconscious; the instinct for ownership that, now or later, lobbies in low key for assimilation or that takes the form of the crude assimilationism of the ugly Puerto Rican, will wreck the movement of the United States of North America to supplant Puerto Rico, to usurp Puerto Rico, to simulate Puerto Rico, to swallow up Puerto Rico. Unless it takes the cures that follow all indigestion.

We Have Run into the Nation

A nation is convergence in space. Such a brief, laconic definition could dislocate the spectacle of verbal immolation that the mere mention of the words *nation, nationality, national* tempts us to. But such a constrained definition is satisfied with what is said openly or suggested: if a nation is convergence in space, it is made up of people affected by it and moved to action by the experiences they share there; experiences, ways of living, the reasonable weight of feeling, the bittersweetness of self-discovery, one's own face discovered among dates and memories that border on oblivion, experiences that the passing of the years filters, fixes, repeats in different, similar, identical ways until they are bound up into signs of identity, signs that are scattered, recovered, put into relief, perpetuated in the portrait of the nation that is its culture.

I do not speak of the culture that finds shelter in the illuminations that the poem transcribes, the culture that one seeks in the colors that move out from a painting, or of that other pleasurably current culture that peoples empty space with syncopated interrogations their own bodies dispel—the culture of the dance that has soared to optimum quality in the United States of North America. I speak of the street, I speak of the people who live and suffer the street, I speak of the people who are born every day, live every day, die every day as Anatole France said—only better. I speak of the culture that people inherit, modify, and pass on.

Provincial—for Metropolitan San Juan is the soma of a sickly adolescent, with its foundations in hybrid Antilleanism and courted by North American fashions and models—consumerism, the little mortgaged house, the indispensable automobile—a jalopy or a cheap little car will do—and other persistent urbanisms, yet modest in their surroundings in Puerto Rican culture. And it is dependent on the focus, prestige, and glamor that North American culture exports—a dependence matched in a significant portion of the cultures of the rest of the world: the jeans that are practical because they are sloppy, or is it the other way round?, the endorsement of the hamburger that you eat with your hands and that abolishes table settings and manners, the cocacolanization of the palate, the youthfulizing asexuality of openness, the powerful abandonment of Tina Turner, the tomorrowism. But although it is provincial, modest, dependent, and other often-repeated diminutions, this is the culture of the Puerto Rican nation, a Hispano-American nation staggering between sleight of hand and limitations, and most of all the recurring doubt as to whether its experience and profundity add up to a nation, form a personality; a Puerto Rican nation interdicted by both natives and foreigners, even though the interdiction did not cut short the journey that affirmed its being as it reached the age of 200, the same 200 years of creative, aggressive independence that is celebrated each Fourth of July by the United States of North America with a legitimate display of pride, confidence, and nationalism.

One Hundred Years of Resistant Solitude

That centuries-old identity gives the lie to the prejudiced and much-anthologized story that the Puerto Ricans are a people who boldly negotiate their own suicide, that the bells already toll for the precariousness of their Spanish language, that the sound of drunkenness and unbridled, astonishing revelry is where their slight intellect and sensitivity reside: an old brothel that capers through linguistic promiscuity, drunken orgies, and simply not being whatever it was she said she was. That cultural identity, based on a provincial, modest, dependent culture, was confirmed when the last century died and the Spanish Empire went all to hell. Beyond hell the Taíno Indians were exterminated a couple of centuries earlier: the Taínos out forever. Here, closer to hell, in hell itself—can they be hell?—the blacks established themselves: the blacks in forever.

And then what was Puerto Rican prevailed against the North American assault: it was never so Puerto Rican as when the North Americans came in through the port of Guanica and the news got around that some *others* were taking over. The Spaniards and the North Americans were always the *others!* Although they were armed with the Spanish language that the Spaniards had rented to them, the Puerto Ricans responded to North American interference. And they resisted the incomprehension and the solitude of almost one hundred years of discordant coupling with the United States of North America: a relationship that cannot be diagrammed, that is supported by a certain mutual scorn, a certain admiration for the "American way of life" on the part of even the most rabid critics of the United States of North America in Puerto Rico, a certain struggle to survive the relationship, to take advantage of its benefits and protect oneself from harm. Opportunism, intimidation, conviction, lying in ambush: a quartet of self-fertilizing tensions interpret the dissonant melody of the Puerto Rican nation, the Puerto Rican colony.

Grand Finale

Honestly and manipulatively, who in the world is not sometimes honest and sometimes manipulative? I am speaking about adapting and adopting "Don't cry for me Argentina" and releasing it, like weeds that fight the weedkiller, into those altars that in Puerto Rico are jukeboxes; I am speaking, really, of importing it with the *local* title "Don't cry for me Puerto Rico."

Importation at all costs is another sign of the colony. The colony imports even what it honestly doesn't need. What is worse, most of the time the colony imports the absolutely worst available elsewhere: unproductive articles, worn out ideas, despairing people, specialists in how to drink coconut milk, in how to pluck a mature guinea hen, in how to travel standing on a bus, in how to tie your shoes. The persistent dynamic of the colony is to declare the incompetence of the natives, the *locals*. Puerto Rico is a colony that is a nation that is a colony. One conveys the other: Puerto Rico is the great Antillean market, the footbridge over which parade all kinds of merchandise, mannequins, orphans. The crude call it *"The Great Cabaret."* The effusive call it *"The New and Shining Batista's Cuba."*

Sad News

Puerto Rico is the bitter country we have made or have allowed to be made bitter for us. Puerto Rico today, Puerto Rico right now, is the country that authorized our spiritual unemployment. Without beating around the bush, the suggested importation, adaptation, and massification by jukebox of the British tango, its jibarification into "Don't cry for me, Puerto Rico," are the vulnerable masks of a witticism to which you recite "Bonjour, tristesse"— and out falls Paul Elouard.

And the country of Puerto Rico, tempestuous in its confusion, assaulted by self-devouring violence—pathetic violence without promise—divided into three hostile denouements, Puerto Rico is a country that pushes its way toward sorrow. And embarrassment: the flagrant lie of the posters that invite participation in the Fourth of July parade in San Juan. But crying is a task that distracts you and puts you out of work. Sorrow—I don't know. A hypothesis, more or less: shall I write don't cry for me, Puerto Rico, or shall I write I don't cry for you?

Americas Society Conference Program: Public Information and the Political Status of Puerto Rico

Reception with The Honorable Hernán Padilla, Former Mayor of San Juan, Puerto Rico

Introduction by Russell E. Marks, Jr., Former President, Americas Society

Welcome by David Rockefeller, Chairman, Americas Society

"Puerto Rico in an International Context," former Mayor Hernán Padilla

"Importance of Puerto Rico in National Politics," Prepared by The Honorable Maurice Ferre, Former Mayor of Miami, Florida, and read by Ambassador Loren Lawrence, Former Senior Fellow, Americas Society

Conclusion by Martha T. Muse, Chairman and President, The Tinker Foundation

"An Historical and Analytical Overview of the Political Status of Puerto Rico," Jeffrey Puryear, Representative, Southern Cone and Andean Zone, The Ford Foundation

Economic Issues Part I: "Investment and Economic Development in Puerto Rico," José R. Madera Prado, Former Director, Economic Development Administration, FOMENTO

Presiding: Russell E. Marks, Jr., Former President, Americas Society

The Honorable Rafael Hernández Colón, Governor of Puerto Rico, "Puerto Rico and the PDP Position: Commonwealth"

Introduction by Arthur M. Schlesinger, Jr., Albert Schweitzer Chair, City University of New York

Economic Issues Part II: "Puerto Rico and the CBI," Stephen Lande, Manchester Associates

Nelson Famadas, Former Economic Advisor, Office of the Governor of Puerto Rico

Presiding: Ambassador Loren Lawrence, Former Senior Fellow, Americas Society

"Federal Policy and Puerto Rico's Political Development," José R. Madera Prado, Former Director, Economic Development Administration, FOMENTO

Commentary: José Villamil, Centro para Estudios de la Realidad Puertorriqueña (CEREP)

The Honorable Carlos Romero Barceló, Former Governor of Puerto Rico, "Puerto Rico and the PNP Position: Statehood"

Introduction by Glenn C. Bassett, Jr., Former Vice-President, Americas Society

Presiding: Theodore C. Sorenson, Paul, Weiss, Rifkind, Wharton and Garrison

"Press Coverage of Puerto Rico," Juan Manuel García Passalacqua, Columnist, *San Juan Star,* and George McDougall, Former Special Assistant, Office of the Governor of Puerto Rico

The Honorable Rubén Berríos Martínez, Senator, Head of Puerto Rican Independence Party, "Puerto Rico and the PIP Position: Independence"

Introduction by Ambassador Loren Lawrence, Former Senior Fellow, Americas Society

International Issues: "The United Nations and Immigration," Marcia Rivero Quintero, Centro para Estudios de la Realidad Puertorriqueña (CEREP), and Francisco Catalá, Puerto Rican Independence Party

Presiding: Christopher Mitchell, Chairman, Department of Political Science, and Director of Center for Latin American and Caribbean Studies, New York University

Concluding Statements: Pamela S. Falk, Associate Director, Institute of Latin American and Iberian Studies, Columbia University, and Former Director of Latin American Affairs, Americas Society

Concert with Yomo Toro y Su Conjunto

Americas Society Puerto Rico Project:

Pamela S. Falk, Director

Lauretta Cohen, Program Associate

Gabrielle S. Brussel, Research Associate and Production Manager, *Puerto Rico's Political Status*

Acknowledgments

A mong the most complex issues for U.S. policymakers and the most hotly debated issue for residents of Puerto Rico is the relationship of the island and the mainland in U.S. national politics. Compiling an anthology that seeks to represent all three political parties and their views on the political status debate was a difficult and rewarding segment of the Americas Society/Center for Inter-American Relations Puerto Rico Project.

Scores of experts, politicians, academics, and business executives helped us sort through the maze of information and issues that are involved in the debate; even vocabulary as simple as *immigration* or *emigration, island* or *country* may shape a statement in favor of one political option or another. We are grateful to the staffs of all three political parties represented in this book—the Popular Democratic Party, the New Progressive Party, and the Puerto Rican Independence Party—for their assistance in obtaining the participation of the party heads. For special help with current statistics and development information, we thank the Economic Development Administration of Puerto Rico (FOMENTO), which has been particularly cooperative during two separate administrations. Special thanks go to Ms. Magda Aguilar and Ms. Estela Ruaño. We are grateful to artist Ignacio Gómez for creating a jacket design and especially to author Luis Rafael Sánchez for his foreword. We regret that space considerations forced us to severely limit the length of most of the articles. The conference participants are listed within the book, but we are also indebted to and extend a special thank you to presiders Martha T. Muse, Arthur M. Schlesinger, Jr., and Theodore C. Sorenson for their contributions to the conference. Finally, we thank all the news writers, editors, and producers who attended the seminar.

As this was a four-year, two-part project, several people were involved in early and later segments of the proposal at the Americas Society. Russell E. Marks, Jr., under whose presidency the project was carried out, made the project possible. Thanks should also go to Ambassador George W. Landau and to Roger Stone and Ronald Hellman.

Without conference staff, a three-day seminar would have been impossible. For devotion and very long hours, I thank Lauretta Cohen, project associate and administrative coordinator of the Latin American Affairs Program, and several student interns: Stephen Gaulle, Jennifer Moore, Eduardo Cuesta, and Dora Plavatic.

The principal contributor to the production of the book was Gabrielle Brussel, a graduate student in international affairs at Columbia University, who was the research associate for the project and the Americas Society's production manager for the book and who spent long yet fruitful hours obtaining copies of legislation on Puerto Rico for the appendixes, researching economic and political data, and helping to get all aspects of the book into production, even long after she had left the Americas Society for full-time graduate studies. We also thank Thelma and Alisa Brussel for their help with the preparation of the manuscript. The concert that was presented at the conclusion of the conference, "Yomo Toro y Su Conjunto," was produced by the Performing Arts Department of the Center—Lucille Duncan, director—with additional funding provided by Verna Gillis's *Soundscape* and cosponsored by the Consolidated Edison of New York and funded through a grant from *Meet the Composer*. Most important, we thank Beatrice Wolfe, Octavio Velázquez, and Mackey Browne, without whose direction and devotion no program is possible at the Americas Society.

Lexington Books has been dedicated throughout the production process, and we thank Jamie Welch-Donahue, Karen Storz, Richard Tonachel, Eileen Young, Karen E. Maloney, Mary Winsley, and the staff at Lexington Books, D.C. Heath and Company.

Without generous funding from several foundations, the project would not have been possible. The Americas Society and the Center for Inter-American Relations thank the Ford Foundation, division of Caribbean affairs, the Angel Ramos Foundation, and the Tinker Foundation—and their respective presidents, Mr. Franklin Thomas, Mrs. Argentina Hills, and Miss Martha Muse—for funding different aspects of the project.

Part I
Background of the Debate

1

Puerto Rico: An American Dilemma

Jeffrey Puryear
Representative, Southern Cone and Andean Zone,
The Ford Foundation

T he United States' 88-year-old relationship with Puerto Rico has become outdated, and the chief obstacles to change now lie in Washington rather than in San Juan. For 30 years, conventional wisdom has maintained that Puerto Ricans are free to alter their relationship with the United States whenever they wish, and thus the next steps are up to them. However, Puerto Rico's remarkably democratic political system is divided and demoralized after years of fruitless battle over whether the island should remain a commonwealth of the United States, seek statehood, or become independent. Prospects for consensus on the status issue have significantly increased but are stalled by Washington's unwillingness to signal what kinds of changes it will permit. Growing pressure for a plebiscite on the status issue could soon produce a simple majority in favor of statehood, leaving Washington unprepared and compelled to act. Simultaneously, comment in the United Nations and at gatherings of Latin American political parties increasingly charges the United States with colonialism and calls for Puerto Rican independence. It is time for Washington to reexamine its fundamental assumptions about Puerto Rico and to establish in Congress an ongoing body that can air diverse viewpoints on Puerto Rico's political status, seek consensus, and address the island's pressing economic problems.

Once a model of self-help development for other nations, Puerto Rico's "Operation Bootstrap" has become consumption-oriented and dependent on the federal government. The economy is in a severe recession, with unemployment at 20 percent, more than half the population receiving food stamps, and federal transfer payments growing rapidly. Puerto Ricans continue to be second-class citizens, subject to the dictates of Congress but without a vote in congressional or presidential elections. The United States has regularly misunderstood Puerto Rico's problems and has often neglected them. The Caribbean Basin Initiative (CBI), which advocates economic development policies for the rest of the Caribbean similar to those of Puerto Rico, is a recent and ironic example. By extending to other Caribbean countries Puerto Rico's free access to U.S. markets, the CBI decreases the island's competitiveness and aggravates its economic problems.

At least three fundamental misconceptions contribute to the present stalemate. First, Washington tends to misconstrue the problem as one of self-determination. In fact, however, the chief problem is Puerto Rico's political and economic dependence on Washington. Until Washington addresses that problem, by advising Puerto Rico of the kinds of conditions that Washington might attach to a change in status, self-determination cannot take place. Second, mainland observers have recently maintained that it's up to Puerto Rico to initiate change in its relationship with the United States. In fact, Puerto Rico has suggested specific changes to Congress at least twice during the past 20 years and has been rebuffed on both occasions. Because Washington has been unwilling to respond to Puerto Rico's initiatives, it has the responsibility for setting in motion fundamental changes. Third, debate has focused on which of the three status options (statehood, a revised commonwealth, or independence) is most desirable. In fact, these outcomes have different meanings to different people, rendering such debate fruitless. The emphasis now should be on process rather than on product. Washington should initiate an ongoing process that can regularly bring together those interested in Puerto Rico's status, clarify underlying issues, and slowly build consensus.

A History of Inattention

History is a good place to start. Today's uncertainty about Puerto Rico's political status derives from a fateful decision in 1898 to alter the traditional purpose for which the United States acquired territory. Previously, territories were acquired on the assumption that they would eventually become states.[1] The territorial clause of the Constitution explicitly gives Congress the power to admit new states into the union and broad authority over territories belonging to the United States.[2] Territories were embryonic states that required nurture to prepare them for full statehood. They were held for no other reason. Thus the Constitution, and subsequently the courts, had been willing to uphold broad discretionary powers by the Congress and Executive over territories, so long as statehood was the goal and reasonable progress was made toward achieving it.

This pattern changed in 1898. Puerto Rico was acquired by the United States from Spain, along with Guam and the Philippines, in the "splendid little war." The 1898 Treaty of Paris made no mention of statehood, and the Foraker Act of 1900, the first of three acts defining relations between the United States and Puerto Rico, in effect made the island a dependent ward of the U.S. Congress, without the full guarantees of the U.S. Constitution accorded to the states and with no promise that statehood would ever be granted. A civil government based on a strong Hamiltonian executive appointed by Washington was established. Although a locally elected House of Delegates was set up, [Congress reserved the right to declare null and void any laws passed by the Puerto Rican Congress and to specify which U.S. laws would not apply to Puerto Rico.] For the first time in its history, the United States acted as a colonial power, acquiring territory by treaty with no promise, direct or implicit, of eventual statehood.[3]

Not surprisingly, the action was widely debated in the United States and was challenged in the Supreme Court in a group of decisions known as the "Insular Cases."[4] In one of the great debates in the history of U.S. constitutional law, the court broke with the traditional territory-state dichotomy and devised a new distinction between incorporated and unincorporated territories. In *Downes v. Bidwell* and *Dorr v. the United States,* the court declared that the fundamental guarantees of the Constitution applied only to "incorporated" territories. If a territory was "unincorporated"—that is, not formally intended to become a state according to the terms of its acquisition—Congress was found to have the power to determine which parts of the Constitution would apply to that territory. This distinction enabled the court to declare an anomalous status for the newly acquired territories, in which the normal constitutional restraints on executive and congressional power did not apply. [This departure from American egalitarian traditions constitutes the root of Puerto Rico's status problems today.]

The subsequent history of Puerto Rico has involved the gradual expansion of local self-government, but without disturbing the fundamentally dependent relationship between the island and the mainland. The Jones Act of 1917 marked a substantial step toward home rule, establishing a bill of rights that included all the guarantees of the U.S. Constitution (except the right to indictment by grand jury and the right to trial by jury), expanding local government, and extending citizenship to all Puerto Ricans who desired it (thereby making Puerto Ricans subject to the military draft). Yet Puerto Rico remained an unincorporated territory, and Congress retained the right to nullify any local law.

[In a series of measures beginning in 1947 and culminating in 1952 in the Federal Relations Act, Congress authorized Puerto Rico to organize a constitutional government. As a result, a constitution was devised and adopted by Puerto Rican delegates, leading to a popularly elected governor, a bicameral legislature, and a local governmental system remarkably similar to those of the 50 states. Federal responsibility in purely local matters was terminated, and local executive, legislative, and judicial authority rested with Puerto Rico. The result, designated an *estado libre asociado* or "commonwealth," had several peculiar characteristics, including exemption from U.S. income taxes, free trade with the United States, a continuation of U.S. citizenship, freedom of movement between the island and the mainland, and access to many of the social services offered by the U.S. government.]

However, the fundamental relationship between Puerto Rico and the

United States did not change. Puerto Ricans still cannot vote in presidential elections (although the political parties now include them in presidential primaries) and have no vote in the U.S. Congress. They are represented instead by a popularly elected resident commissioner, who can introduce legislation and speak in the House of Representatives but cannot vote on the House floor. Moreover, Puerto Rico's participation in the programs of the federal government depends on congressional decision rather than on the rights to equal treatment under the laws guaranteed by the U.S. Constitution. Puerto Rico is subject to the dictates of Congress without having a vote to influence congressional decisions.

Thus, Puerto Rico was accorded neither the full protection of the U.S. Constitution nor the promise of statehood that had applied to all previous territories. Instead, it became the consequence of a departure in America's approach to annexing territories and formalized a basic contradiction between democracy and empire in this country's history. The relationship is fundamentally colonial and hardly equitable, even though it has been marked by the generosity and good intentions of Washington and the consent of many Puerto Ricans.[7]

Yet few in the United States have been able to see it that way. As a nation based on equality and independence, the United States has found it painful to acknowledge this imperial strain in its history. Instead, this country has superficially defined the problem of Puerto Rico's status in terms of self-determination. Ambassador Jeane Kirkpatrick's statement was typical: "The people of Puerto Rico . . . are free to reconsider the nature of their relationship with the United States at any time."[8]

Although this approach may be valid for relationships among equals—such as hold between two sovereign nations—it is invalid in dependent situations. Puerto Rico is not free to determine its future relationships with the mainland because it has relatively little power to act on its preferences. Regardless of what Puerto Rico wants, Washington will ultimately decide what Puerto Rico gets. Thus, the central issue facing policymakers regarding Puerto Rico is not self-determination but dependence. Until the United States addresses the unequal nature of the relationship, self-determination cannot take place.

If Puerto Rico's dependence on Washington is the central issue, then it follows that the initiative to change Puerto Rico's political status must come from the mainland. Puerto Rico has the right to help determine its future political status, but the mainland currently has most of the power. There is a paradox here that derives from the fundamentally unequal nature of the relationship between the island and the mainland. Each of the options facing the island—statehood, a revised commonwealth status, and independence—might be attractive to Puerto Ricans, depending on the conditions attached to them. That is the problem: Only Congress can spell out the conditions. Washington maintains that it doesn't know what Puerto Rico wants, yet what Puerto Rico wants depends on what Washington is willing to grant.

Suppose, for example, a plebiscite were held and statehood (or any other option) won. What next? Puerto Rico would expect Congress to act in good faith and begin deliberations leading to a vote on Puerto Rico's petition for statehood. Yet public opinion on the mainland is woefully uninformed about Puerto Rico and unprepared to make decisions on the complex issues a change in Puerto Rico's status would raise. Becoming properly prepared for those decisions will take time, and it should not be delayed until the United States is confronted with an urgent (and perhaps nonnegotiable) request from Puerto Rico.

The Stalemate

The current stalemate underscores one more misconception—that debate should be over which of the three status options is "best." In fact, such debate has been fruitless and has often diverted attention from crucial assumptions and important underlying issues. The emphasis now should be on process rather than on product. Washington should establish a systematic and ongoing process that includes all major Puerto Rican political interests and can air competing viewpoints, clarifying underlying issues, educate mainland public opinion, and slowly help build consensus.

The argument for establishing such a process rests on several facts. First, the United States' growing interest in the Caribbean—represented by the Caribbean Basin Initiative—has thus far left Puerto Rico out. Yet the island's economic problems, unresolved political status, and Latin character all bring risks for a United States seeking to expand its influence in the region. The CBI includes no steps to ameliorate these risks and even promises to aggravate them by extending Puerto Rico's tariff concessions to other Caribbean countries. It is thus prudent for the United States to address existing problems before they become crises, thereby demonstrating its determination to be a good citizen in a region concerned about the sudden interest of its northern neighbor.

Second, the status options available to Puerto Rico have not yet been defined. Each of the options commonly mentioned—statehood, a revised commonwealth, or independence—could have a variety of characteristics attached to them that are crucial in determining their desirability.[9] Thus much of the debate so far has been illusory, because those involved have had different definitions of a single status option and because no one knows which of those definitions has any real chance of winning approval. Until crucial issues have been clarified and real options identified, debate on status options is largely meaningless.

Third, economic issues are most important. The success of Operation Bootstrap has always depended on the combination of federal and local tax exemptions, privileged access to the U.S. market, and cheap, good-quality labor.[10] That formula worked until the mid-1960s, when the Kennedy round of tariff reductions began to cut into Puerto Rico's comparative advantage, federal minimum wage laws were gradually applied to the island, and federal environmental standards began to raise local business expenses. The run-up in petroleum prices in the early 1970s and the world recession in the 1980s aggravated Puerto Rico's existing economic difficulties. The Reagan administration's 1981 tax bill, by lowering corporate income taxes and amending the benefits available to corporations operating in Puerto Rico, decreased the island's attraction to mainland capital. Now the Caribbean Basin Initiative, by enlarging the number of countries with duty-free access to the U.S. market and tax exemptions, would further weaken Puerto Rico's comparative advantage.

[As a result, Puerto Rico became increasingly dependent on grants, transfer payments, and services from the federal government.] Between 1970 and 1980, federal transfer payments rose from less than 5 percent of personal income to approximately 30 percent.[11] By 1981, approximately 55 percent of the population was receiving food stamps.[12] Although per capita federal expenditures are still well below those of the 50 states, direct federal assistance to Puerto Rican incomes is higher than in any state because incomes are, on the average, lower in Puerto Rico.

[Fourth, if economics is the biggest barrier to independence, language and culture are the biggest barriers to statehood.] Although Puerto Ricans speak all the English they need to deal effectively with the mainland, Spanish remains their principal language. This is so despite the persistent efforts of U.S. policymakers between 1899 and 1949 to make English the chief language of instruction in the island's schools and 80 years of extensive contact with the mainland. The statehood movement considers the language issue to be nonnegotiable and cites the fact that the U.S. Constitution does not establish an official language for the country. Although statehood advocates fully agree that both languages should be taught in the schools, they insist that the principal language of instruction be Spanish.]

Puerto Ricans favoring other status options tend to agree. Their concern is basically cultural and represents a legitimate fear that statehood will mean losing their Puerto Rican identity. Reports from the mainland on discrimination against Hispanics serve to heighten these fears and strengthen Puerto Rican resolve to defend their identity in the face of middle-class America. Culture is at the heart of Puerto Rican resistance to statehood, and language is its political manifestation.

Yet opinion on the mainland has been sharply divided on the language issue. These divisions have been exacerbated by the recent massive inflows to the United States of monolingual Spanish-speaking immigrants from Mexico and Cuba. The recent sentiment in Miami against bilingualism is symptomatic of a broader unease in the United States over this country's cultural diversity and integration.[13] Although no consensus is apparent, the present debate suggests that a Spanish-speaking Puerto Rican state will not automatically win acceptance. Also, each of the three previous cases in which territories with large non-English-speaking populations were admitted as states (Oklahoma, Arizona, and New Mexico) included the condition that public school classes be conducted in English.[14] Clearly, language (and the cultural concerns it represents) remains a serious and complex issue that requires careful consideration by both sides.

Fifth, those favoring a revised commonwealth arrangement advocate permitting Puerto Rico to enter into bilateral and multilateral treaty relations with neighboring countries and to be represented in at least some international organizations. These arrangements, which are in keeping with the autonomous sentiment behind the commonwealth concept, would counteract charges that Washington's role is basically colonial. Yet their constitutionality is seldom discussed. Similarly, commonwealth advocates suggest that Puerto Rico be allowed to control immigration to the island, so as to prevent the domination by outside groups that already characterizes the Virgin Islands.

Sixth, the issue of citizenship accompanies any consideration of the status option. Puerto Ricans have been U.S. citizens since 1917. Would dual citizenship be possible under an independent Puerto Rico? Could those who already have U.S. citizenship retain it, leaving only the newborn and immigrants to have exclusive Puerto Rican citizenship?

Until these and other issues are clarified and Puerto Ricans know which kind of independence, statehood, or revised commonwealth might be acceptable to Washington, they can hardly be expected to abandon the status quo and develop a consensus on their future.

The Importance of Process

Process is important because the mainland is uninformed about the status issue. The limited debate has been confined to Ad Hoc Committees, Presidential politics and international organizations. Indeed, while debate in these settings helps raise the issue, it does not properly provide for change, and may be harmful.

Presidential involvement in the status debate began in the mid 1970s, when the Democratic party decided to treat Puerto Rico as a state in the nominating convention, even though it may not vote in the presidential election. Today, Presidential candidates from both parties have given the impression that change is Puerto Rico's for the asking. Yet only Congress has the authority to dispose of territory belonging to the United States. Thus, any presidential initiative is still a step away from the locus of decision. And if Puerto Rico were to choose an option different from that favored by the president, how effective could that president be in recommending Puerto Rico's wishes to Congress?

The International Dimension

During the 1970s, international interest in Puerto Rico's status began to grow, aided by a general trend among Latin American countries to adopt more assertive foreign policies vis-à-vis the United States. The Permanent Conference of Latin American Political Parties (COPPAL), a collection of Social-Democratic parties, has voted on several occasions in favor of independence for Puerto Rico.[15] Although many of the parties represented in COPPAL are small, they include influential groups—such as Mexico's ruling party, the *Partido Revolucionario Institucional* (PRI), Colombia's *Liberal* party, *Acción Democrática* of Venezuela, and the *Alianza Popular Revolucionaria Americana* (APRA) of Peru. Similarly, the Socialist International voted unanimously in November 1982 to support the Puerto Rican Independence Party in its fight for Puerto Rican independence.[16]

Perhaps most important, the United Nations Special Committee on Decolonization recommended in 1981, for the first time since Puerto Rico was removed from the list of non-self-governing territories in 1953, that Puerto Rico's relationship with the United States be debated in the General Assembly. Although the proposal (sponsored by Cuba) and a similar one in 1982 were later defeated in the General Assembly, their approval in committee after being rejected for several years illustrates the growing willingness of many countries to challenge the official opinion of the United States. The voting patterns in 1982 were significant. Two long-standing allies of the United States—Venezuela and Argentina—voted for the proposal, and several others—including Peru, Mexico, the Dominican Republic, and Spain—abstained. In early 1983, a group of nations preparing for the meetings of the Non-Aligned Movement in New Delhi agreed to include Puerto Rico's political status on the agenda. During the next few years, the status issue may well become something of a lightning rod for Latin American countries that wish to demonstrate their independence from the United States in the wake of the Falklands/Malvinas conflict.

The Locus of Decision

The United States has never developed a proper setting for debating Puerto Rico's status. As Gordon Lewis has cogently pointed out: "The management of empire by a democracy is a contradiction in terms."[17] The libertarian and egalitarian principles that dominate the U.S. self-concept have made it difficult to establish the formal machinery necessary to govern territories like Puerto Rico appropriately.

Today, no central focus of authority exists that can address the fundamental differences between Puerto Rico and the 50 states and channel consultation between island institutions and federal headquarters. Instead, the U.S. national government addresses Puerto Rico much as it would a state. Many mainland institutions with a stake in the island's status—including the U.S. Navy (which has highly prized bases in Puerto Rico) and many private corporations (which benefit from the tax exemptions currently associated with operating on the island)—pursue their interests through separate avenues to the federal government. Various departments of the executive branch—such as Interior, Agriculture, Commerce, and Defense—have direct responsibilities and interests in the island. Yet the level and composition of federal expenditures is determined separately by Congress, rather than by the constitutional guarantees that apply to the other 50 states. The result has been divided authority, divided responsibility, and a failure to monitor systematically and understand comprehensively changes in Puerto Rico.

The absence of a proper focus of authority in Washington has also made it more difficult for Puerto Ricans to reach agreement. Although the pro-statehood forces won their first gubernatorial election in 1968, electoral advantage has alternated since then between the pro-commonwealth Popular Democratic Party and the pro-statehood New Progressive Party, with the Independence Party trailing significantly behind but holding a pivotal percentage. The status debate is monopolizing the democratic political system in Puerto Rico and discrediting it for not making progress on other pressing problems. A poll commissioned by a local newspaper revealed that nearly two-thirds of Puerto Rican voters rejected the candidacy of both leaders of the island's two major political parties in the 1984 gubernatorial election and that three-quarters believed that only a minority of Puerto Rican politicians were honest.[18] This growing frustration with democratic politics is particularly disturbing in a society that is perhaps the most well-educated, politically active, and democratic in Latin America and has averaged a voter turnout of 85 percent since 1920.

There is remarkable agreement, however, among Puerto Rican leaders that the present situation is intolerable and that change must occur. In late 1981, a commission was established to resolve the dilemma of Puerto Rico's political status; the commission was composed of representatives of each of the island's three major political parties. The proper setting for this initiative is probably Congress. Only Congress can dispose of U.S. territories, and Congress will ultimately have to decide what conditions attach to any change. Also, because the issues involved are diverse and will not be quickly resolved, they require attention that is more balanced and sustained than the rhythm of presidential politics is likely to provide. Presidents can advocate, but Congress will have to analyze and decide.

From the viewpoint of U.S. national interests, one promising approach might be for Congress to establish a joint committee on Puerto Rico. A joint congressional committee, with an appropriate professional staff, would have the continuity and expertise necessary to sift through the complex array of arguments and issues associated with the status problem, to air diverse viewpoints, and to seek consensus. Although a joint committee would not propose status changes—only a mechanism that includes the Puerto Rican political parties should do that—it could clarify underlying issues, help Congress determine the conditions it might attach to status alternatives, and begin to educate mainland groups.

The committee would act as the focal point for debate and coordination on Puerto Rican issues. Its staff would be professional and would have qualifications commensurate with the broad range of social and economic issues that are central to United States–Puerto Rico relations. It would make recommendations regarding all congressional and executive treatment of the island, including appropriations, application of federal regulations, and steps toward status change. It would regularly hear the views of all island and mainland groups that have an interest in Puerto Rico's relationship with the United States. In addition to review and educational functions, the committee should have the mandate and resources to carry out specific tasks designed to facilitate any change in Puerto Rico's status.

A study of voting behavior in Puerto Rico should also be undertaken to determine the conditions under which a plebiscite or referendum could be considered a legitimate reflection of Puerto Rican preferences. Several aspects of Puerto Rican politics, including the traditionally high voter turnout and the primacy of economic and cultural issues in determining status preferences, must be understood in advance of any referendum on status change. Studies of Puerto Rico's economic prospects under different relationships with the mainland are also important. The 1979 Kreps report, prepared by the Department of Commerce, deliberately avoided such analysis. Existing material is minimal and often rhetorical. Neither Puerto Rico nor the mainland has solid information on the economic options open to the island.[19]

Most important, such a committee should exist until such time as Puerto Rico either becomes independent or is granted statehood. Any other status is by nature arbitrary and dependent, legitimated neither by the constitutional guarantees of statehood nor by the freedom that accompanies independence. It therefore requires constant monitoring to ensure that responsibilities are properly discharged and that changes are made when appropriate.

Once the issues have been clarified and Congress has begun to develop informed opinions on them, a joint United States–Puerto Rico commission, with representation from all Puerto Rican political parties, could be established to discuss procedures for changing the legal and political relationship between the island and the mainland. Over a period of several years, this group might then carry out the negotiation and education that are necessary for a satisfactory and enduring solution. The real promise for productive change lies in seeking agreement over prolonged periods on specific issues while continuing education and debate on the rest.

Toward a Satisfactory Solution

Before a plebiscite could play a useful role, alternatives must be explored, relevant groups must be educated, international legitimacy must be created, and consensus must be built. Only then could a plebiscite help resolve the complex issues underlying the status problem.

Priority now should be on recognizing that Puerto Rico needs attention, that change is under way, and that the United States has both an interest in and a responsibility for bringing change about. Democracies have rarely divested themselves gracefully of colonial possessions precisely because having those possessions contradicts the fundamental values of democracies. By deliberately establishing a mechanism for reviewing change in Puerto Rico's status, Congress might rescue the issue. It would also demonstrate to the world that the United States is willing to tackle Caribbean problems that involve a critical look at ourselves as well as those that involve the East-West conflict.

Notes

1. The debatable exception was Alaska, purchased from Russia in 1867. In 1905, the Supreme Court ruled that Alaska was "an incorporated territory," thereby implying that eventual statehood had been intended.

2. U.S. Constitution, art. IV, par. 3, clauses 1 and 2.

3. Henry Wells, *The Modernization of Puerto Rico* (Cambridge, Massachusetts: Harvard University Press, 1969), pp. 82–86; Gordon Lewis, *Freedom and Power in the Caribbean* (New York: Monthly Review Press, 1963), pp. 106–12.

4. Lewis, *Freedom and Power,* pp. 109–10.

5. In subsequent decisions, the court applied this distinction to other cases, finding Hawaii and the Philippines to be unincorporated but Alaska to be incorporated.

6. The most recent Supreme Court case upholding the congressional power to treat Puerto Rico differently from the states is Harris v. Rosario, 446 U.S. 651, 656 (1980) (Marshall, J., dissenting); the decision is discussed in David C. Indiano and Harry A. Cook, "Recent Decision," *Case Western Reserve Journal of International Law* 12(Summer 1980):641–51.

7. The issue of colonialism is explored in Lewis, *Freedom and Power*, pp. 69–84, 409–37; and in Jose A. Cabranes, "Puerto Rico out of the Colonial Closet," *Foreign Policy,* Winter 1981:66–91.

8. Press Release USUN 67 (82), United States Mission to the United Nations, 22 September 1982; Under Secretary of Interior Pedro San Juan put it more succinctly during a recent visit to the Virgin Islands when he said: "The . . . United States is not a colonial state and never has been." *San Juan Star,* 22 January 1983.

9. This problem is elaborated in United States General Accounting Office, *Puerto Rico's Political Future: A Divisive Issue with Many Dimensions,* GGD–81–48 (Washington, D.C.: Government Printing Office, 2 March 1981).

10. U.S. Department of Commerce, *Economic Study of Puerto Rico* (Washington, D.C.: Government Printing Office, December 1979), Part I, p. 9.

11. Puerto Rico Planning Board, *Statistical Appendix to the Economic Report to the Governor for FY 1981.* (San Juan: Government Development Bank for Puerto Rico, 1981).

12. Marianne Hill, "The Nutrition Assistance Program in Puerto Rico: Present Impact and Proposed Changes," *Puerto Rico Business Review* 7(July-August 1982):4.

13. The views of Senator Simpson (R-Wyoming), co-author of the Simpson-Mazzoli bill on immigration policy, strongly support the "one nation, one language" approach.

14. Comptroller General of the United States, *Experiences of Past Territories Can Assist Puerto Rico Status Deliberation,* GGD–80–26 (Washington, D.C.: General Accounting Office, 1980), p. 14.

15. COPPAL, Declaration of La Paz, Bolivia, October 1982, and Declaration of Oaxaca, 10 October 1979.

16. Socialist International, General Circular No. 63/82, 10 November 1982.

17. Lewis, *Freedom and Power*, p. 122.

18. *El Nuevo Día,* 5 November 1982.

19. For a useful step in this direction, see Bertram Finn, "The Economic Implications of Statehood for Puerto Rico: A Preliminary Analysis," Unpublished paper prepared for a workshop, "The United States and Puerto Rico," organized by the Latin American Program of the Woodrow Wilson International Center for Scholars, Washington, D.C., 16–18 April 1980.

2
Puerto Rico: Its Dilemma and Its Destiny

The Honorable Baltasar Corrada del Río
Mayor of San Juan

On July 25, 1898, American troops landed in Puerto Rico. Eighty-eight years later, the problem of the political status of Puerto Rico has not been definitely resolved. Despite the milestones of our century, political leaders in Puerto Rico still debate the political formulas that leaders at the turn of the century debated. More surprisingly, there are some who still argue that Puerto Rico should remain in this pervasive political limbo, that we need more time to decide. Although the world has been reshaped, reconstructed, and rebuilt more than once in our time, the island remains stagnant with a political status of ambiguity and indecision.

Decades ago, it would have been possible to explain or even justify why political leaders remained somewhat ambiguous concerning the status question. Social and economic problems were indeed severe in the 1930s and 1940s. The world was recovering from the worst economic depression of our times and preparing for a major war. Statehood for noncontiguous U.S. territories was not foreseeable, and independence was impractical. Under such circumstances, it could be understood why political leaders wanted to postpone a decision on Puerto Rico's political status.

Today, after 88 years of debates, experiments, and experiences, the people of Puerto Rico must turn to political definition. The ambivalence of commonwealth *(estado libre asociado)* as a political status has allowed for the division of the people of Puerto Rico into three separate political ideologies. This fragmentation represents a profound impediment for the unity of our people—a unity that is essential to achieve the kind of environment conducive to a higher order of economic and social progress. The "institutionalization" of a society sharply divided in three segments has contributed to a highly politicized atmosphere in which it is much more difficult to tackle serious economic and social problems.

The theory that commonwealth status was to provide for a middle-ground between the two extremes—independence and statehood—has proved to be a great fallacy. Commonwealth is the main cause of our divisions. Commonwealth is the problem. The real unity and solidarity of our people will come when our political status is definitely and finally resolved. That final decision should be at the top of the agenda of our people and of all responsible Puerto Rican political leaders. Thirty-one years of commonwealth status have left us convinced that, today more than ever, we need to find something better, more dignified, and more definitive.

It is incumbent upon us to propose a viable, favorable, and patriotic alternative for the solution of the Puerto Rican dilemma: a solution that allows our people to exercise their full political rights, maximize their economic development, and promote better social conditions; a solution that propends toward the preservation and enrichment of our culture, language, and identity. This alternative is statehood, under specific favorable conditions to be attained in the enabling act.

Statehood means political integration, not cultural assimilation, of Puerto Rico with the most powerful nation on Earth: a nation with deep democratic ideals and convictions; a nation that has some defects but is open to ideas and change and has many virtues; a nation committed to freedom and justice.

Puerto Rico has achieved a degree of local self-government with the creation of commonwealth. However, the island lacks adequate political participation at the federal level.

Statehood provides local self-government as well as more political participation in Washington. As a state, Puerto Rico would continue to elect its own governor, as well as senators and representatives to its legislature. In addition, Puerto Ricans would be able to vote in presidential elections and would be afforded equal participation in the U.S. Senate and proportionate representation in the House of Representatives. Puerto Rico's position in the House would be of significant power, since the seven Puerto Rican representatives would give the island more voting power than twenty-six states. This would mean equal and fair treatment in all allocations and appropriations of federal funds for education, health, employment, nutrition, housing, transportation, crime control, general economic development and others: funds not to increase dependency but to promote the economic and social development of the island; funds not to substitute but to complement our efforts to improve our living conditions; funds to be awarded to Puerto Rico not as benevolent handouts but on the basis of need and as a matter of dignity and equality among the states. We will share in the responsibility to pay federal taxes in accordance with our modest means. By giving, we will provide more dignity to our receiving.

The proud character of our people will be enhanced by the new political status. The island will continue to have its two flags and its two anthems— a national flag and anthem and a state flag and anthem. The island will retain its own constitution. Furthermore, our people will benefit from all the rights under the U.S. Constitution, which will apply there *ex propio vigore*, not simply as Congress may wish to extend it to us. Puerto Rico would no longer be under the Territorial Clause of the U.S. Constitution that gives Congress full powers over U.S. territories or possessions. The Territorial Clause is the basic reason why our current status retains the colonial vestiges of political inferiority.

One of the major obstacles regarding the entry of Puerto Rico as a member of the Union is the fear spread by those who oppose statehood that to be a state we must forgo our Puerto Rican culture and language. We can be good Puerto Ricans and good Americans at the same time. The federation of Puerto Rico does not imply the disappearance of our island as a body politic. A state of the Union is a political entity with its own autonomy. Puerto Rico would enjoy the autonomy of a state, not the autonomy of a colony.

Statehood for Puerto Rico would represent a permanent status, not a temporary one. The permanence of that status would bring about the stability and the proper conditions for a higher development of the island's economy.

Puerto Rico would have to negotiate an agreement with Congress to provide certain adjustments and conditions under the statehood enabling act. Some measures concerning the payment of federal taxes after an orderly transition or phase-in period are necessary, considering that as a territory we are not currently paying such taxes. The federal tax credit extended to firms already established on the island could be "grandfathered" for the life of the local grants of tax exemption received by these firms. Vigorous special tax incentives for new firms to invest in Puerto Rico during the initial fifteen or twenty years of statehood could be allowed. Puerto Rico could continue to receive a rebate of federal excise taxes on rum produced by us, so long as the unemployment rate is higher than 10 percent, to create a development fund to promote industry, commerce, agriculture, and education.

The cultural question should be resolved by clear indications that the use of Spanish in Puerto Rico and the preservation of Puerto Rican culture would not be objected to by Congress.

It is not up to Congress to tell us what we should do about our future. Congress will not declare beforehand how far it will go in meeting the demands of the people of Puerto Rico. We must come to Washington with a clear mandate from our people as to what we want. That mandate will, in fact, provide the moral and political support we need to accomplish our ends.

A majority vote from the people of Puerto Rico in favor of statehood is not only a vote in favor of a change in political status. A majority vote in favor of statehood is a vote for the dignity and equality of 3.2 million citizens of the United States who are demanding something to which they are entitled as part of their right to self-determination.

We need a status that assures the maximum political, economic, and social development of Puerto Rico and preserves the identity of our people. That status can be statehood if we manage the issue properly in Congress. Puerto Rico can and should seek, with confidence and trust, full partnership in a nation of dignity, freedom, justice, and prosperity.

3

The State of the Commonwealth, 1985

The Honorable Rafael Hernández Colón
Governor of Puerto Rico
Popular Democratic Party

P lans for change and self-improvement cannot prosper if they are not based on reality. Let us examine the difficult situation in which the island finds itself. Our economy over the past eight years peaked in 1980. It then began to fall, and it has still not recovered completely. During the last fiscal year (1984), the island's adjusted gross product totaled $7 billion, $5 million less than in 1980. The average unemployment rate was 22 percent. Labor participation rate fell to its lowest historical level—42.1 percent. During those eight years, more than 200,000 Puerto Ricans emigrated to the United States in search of opportunities. Real fixed investment, which in 1976 reached $716 million, fell to $466 million in fiscal 1984. These are indications of the steady loss our island's opportunities for progress have suffered over the past eight years. The situation has been complicated by the inefficient administration of Section 936 of the Internal Revenue Code—regarding the creation of jobs—which has led the U.S. Treasury to recommend elimination of this section, the hub of our financial and promotional capabilities. In the current fiscal year, the government has a deficit of $117 million. For the next fiscal year, 1985–86, the previous administration calculated that obligations it had already assumed represented a deficit of $106 million. If we add these incurred obligations, the deficit for 1985–86 increases to $279 million.

The economic situation is very difficult, and that the picture is complicated by a government in deficit, with departments and agencies in total disorganization, with unprecedented corruption, and without a sense of purpose or the will to do anything for our island. During the election campaign and in my inaugural address, I promised the people that I would bring a change that would improve the quality of life of the Puerto Rican people, concentrating on four areas: employment, education, health, and safety. The following programs are our plans for the late 1980's.

Employment

Nothing is more important in creating the Puerto Rico we want than the creation of jobs. The lack of work is a cry of anguish that echoes throughout Puerto Rico. How many times have I heard this cry in the past years—my heart wrenched by the despair of so many Puerto Ricans? The first thing we will do to create jobs will be to stimulate intense construction activity in housing and public works.

Mortgage Trust

In Puerto Rico, the great demand for new housing goes unsatisfied because, with high interest rates, the monthly payments are beyond the means of most Puerto Rican families. We will create a mortgage trust that will combine federal financing programs with Section 936 funds to reduce interest costs to below the prevailing rates.

We will modernize the program of mutual assistance and self-help so that, being given the materials, many families may build their homes with community aid and the technical assistance of the Housing Department. The development of these programs for housing construction will create unusual activity in the construction industry and in commerce, rapidly generating many employment opportunities. In addition, 5,000 lots will be distributed for construction of housing units by the recipients. We will restructure the program of semi-finished housing for young, low-income families, whose homes may be expanded as their income and family needs increase.

Massive Public Works Construction

We propose to increase construction of public works significantly. Conditions in the financial markets are optimal for financing. We will use new financial instruments, which will save us millions of dollars in interest payments on commonwealth and corporative debts. This refinancing will allow us to carry out a broad program of public works construction—using local and federal funds—which will include highways, channeling, sewers, water systems, improvements in telephone service, and other public projects.

Development Bank

Currently less than 5 percent of the assets of the Government Development Bank is lent to the private sector. To offer businesses a source of credit linked to the economic development of the island, thus opening thousands of employment opportunities, we will create a development bank distinct from the Government Development Bank. The Government Development Bank's development functions will be transferred to it, as well as sufficient resources to carry out three basic programs: direct loans, capital participation, and a loan guarantee program. The new development bank will be the organism that—nourished by Section 936 funds—will finance joint projects with Caribbean countries. Thirty-five percent of the labor on these projects will be done in Puerto Rico, creating well-paying jobs for Puerto Ricans. At the same time, production costs will be leveled out by the cheaper labor of other countries.

Manufacturing

We will work toward an industrial renaissance in Puerto Rico. We will put Section 936 to work as it was meant to work—to create jobs. This is the best defense that can be made for that fiscal mechanism. With this industrial renaissance as a goal, I will submit a new industrial incentives act, including total tax exemption for new factories that need it for profitability and that create mass employment.

I will submit legislation to create the position of assistant administrator of FOMENTO for the promotion of Puerto Rican industries, with special attention to be given to native entrepreneurs. The assistant administrator will be appointed by the governor of Puerto Rico and will work closely with the secretary of commerce. With the aim of reducing energy costs, the administration, operation, and finances of the electrical system will be reformed, and the conversion of plants to use coal or oil will be studied in depth. We will experiment with other systems of producing energy—cane and solar energy—and a tax incentive will be offered companies that use alternative energy sources.

Promotional activity will be increased in the industrial centers of the world, and a special effort will be made to attract Japanese manufacturers to Puerto Rico.

Agriculture

The previous administration stressed a few agricultural projects, such as the vegetables and rice project, that required a large investment. A large share of the credit and incentives was given to a handful of firms, to the detriment of thousands of Puerto Rican farmers. We have already begun rigorous evaluation of these projects and have established controls to prevent misuse of public funds.

Commerce

We will facilitate financing to small business through the Commercial Development Company. We will provide legislation authorizing the Commercial Development Company to guarantee loans, up to a maximum of $50 million in each of the next four years, and to provide $30 million in direct loans to be disbursed and administered by the Company.

Look at this picture, not with partisan perspective but with patriotic depth. Paraphrasing that unparalleled Mexican writer, Juan Rulfo, I invite you to reflect dispassionately on this situation, beginning with the true patriotic feeling that faces up to reality and says: This is not the Puerto Rico that we want, but it is the only one we have and love.

Part II
Political Leaders Speak

4

Why Statehood Would Be an Economic Disaster for Puerto Rico

The Honorable Miguel A. Hernández Agosto
President of the Senate of Puerto Rico
Popular Democratic Party

Autonomy under Spain and under the United States

Puerto Rico has always tried to reach a reasonable division of power and obligations in its economic relationship with the metropolis. In 1897, for example, we obtained an autonomous charter from Spain, similar to the present commonwealth status. Unfortunately, the autonomous government created in 1897 lasted only a few months. In July of 1898, the United States declared war on Spain and invaded Puerto Rico, Cuba, and the Phillippines. On December 20, 1898, Puerto Rico—which had already taken the first step from a Spanish colony to a self-governing territory—was thrown back to colonial status under the U.S. flag. This colonial status lasted until 1952, when Puerto Rico again received a measure of autonomous power under the commonwealth status.

The United States and the commonwealth presently share a common defense, market, and currency. The people of Puerto Rico are citizens of the United States and, as such, serve in the armed forces in the same manner as citizens from the rest of the Union. However, they cannot vote in national elections and they are represented in Congress solely by a resident commissioner, who has voice and voting power in congressional committees but only voice on the floor of the House of Representatives.

Most federal taxes, except those, such as social security taxes, that are imposed by mutual consent, are not levied in Puerto Rico. No federal income tax is collected from commonwealth residents on income earned from local sources in Puerto Rico, although federal employees are subject to taxes on their salaries. The subsidiaries of U.S. companies operating in Puerto Rico can, pursuant to Section 936 of the Internal Revenue Code, elect to receive a full credit on their federal taxes on income received from local sources in Puerto Rico. The U.S. parent company also receives a full dividend-received deduction on profits repatriated from its subsidiaries in Puerto Rico.

The Economic Impact of Statehood for Puerto Rico

Statehood for Puerto Rico—using available 1983 statistics—would have the following consequences:

1. Puerto Rico would lose at least 170,000 jobs. This represents 24 percent of all present jobs on the island. The unemployment rate would increase from 23 percent to 42 percent. This loss in jobs would be due primarily to the firms' response to the increase in corporate federal taxes from nil at present to an estimated $1.4 billion yearly under statehood.

2. That enormous loss of jobs, representing nearly a $2 billion loss in salaries and income to the economy, would plunge the island into a depression worse than the one suffered in the late 1920s and early 1930s. This loss of $2 billion in the local economy would represent 19 percent of the net income for 1983.

3. Financial institutions on the island would lose more than $5 billion in Section 936 corporation deposits, equivalent to 40 percent of their present deposits. Some 3,000 jobs would be lost in the financial sector alone. Money would be scarcer, raising interest rates on long-term investments, such as mortgages.

4. Individual federal income taxes would rise from zero at present to some $357 million yearly.

5. Individuals would also have to pay, in addition to federal income taxes, some $172 million in federal excise taxes, including $64 million on alcoholic beverages, $57 million on gasoline, $11 million on cigarettes, and $9 million on telephone service.

6. The commonwealth government would lose $1.4 billion in revenues, equivalent to 48 percent of its revenues during 1983.

7. To close the budgetary gap, the Puerto Rican government would have to fire some 116,000 employees, or 68 percent of those employed in 1983.

8. On the plus side, the Puerto Rican government would receive some $175 million yearly from the U.S. government for general use and $334 million in specific programs. Individuals would receive another $684 million directly from the U.S. government under several federally funded programs.

Thus, the total additional funds that would be received by the state government and individuals from the U.S. government would be approximately $1.2 billion yearly. This amount would be insufficient to cover state and individual losses of nearly $9.3 billion yearly, leaving a gap of $8.2 billion yearly that Puerto Rico would lose under statehood.

The Present Situation under Commonwealth Status

At present, corporations in Puerto Rico do not pay federal income taxes on their local income. This has benefited the island mainly in two ways. First, we have been able to create more jobs. Both Puerto Rican and U.S. firms have created more than 170,000 jobs that would not exist if the firms were subject to federal income taxes.

Second, the commonwealth government has been able to offer essential services to the population by establishing its own state income tax structure. In 1983, the state government received $457 million in corporate income taxes. These were used to pay for education, health, and police protection for the population. If Puerto Rico were a state, its state income taxes would have to be reduced drastically—if not totally eliminated—to accommodate the federal tax burden.

Federal Corporate Income Taxes under Statehood

Should Puerto Rico become a state of the Union and not change its present local taxes, the minimum federal income tax applicable to corporations would be 15 percent of taxable income up to $25,000 yearly. The applicable state tax is 21 percent. Thus, the combined minimum tax burden would be 33.7 percent. The federal income tax increases up to a maximum of 46 percent on income in excess of $100,000 yearly. The present state tax increases to a maximum of 45 percent on income in excess of $300,000. Therefore, the maximum combined tax burden would be a confiscatory 73 percent.

The Tax Burden under Commonwealth Status and under Statehood

What would be the tax burden under statehood as compared to the present tax system? In 1983, the commonwealth government collected a total of $457 million in corporate taxes. Total corporate income in that year was $4.9 billion.

How much would have to be paid in federal taxes under statehood depends on three factors:

1. The effective average federal income tax rate, which in 1983 was 31 percent. This rate is much less than the statutory 46 percent rate because of the various deductions, credits, and accelerated depreciation allowances provided in the federal tax code.

2. The state taxes, which would qualify as a deduction on the federal income tax return.

3. The level of income generated in Puerto Rico, which would certainly change after the change in political status.

If the commonwealth tax structure and the corporate income levels achieved in 1983 were unchanged under statehood, then the corporate federal tax burden under statehood would increase 300 percent, from $457 million to $1.8 billion. This brutal increase in the tax burden of firms operating in Puerto Rico has led many analysts to conclude that under statehood, Puerto Rico would have to reduce its own taxes substantially to accommodate the federal taxes, as the other states have been forced to do.

Thus, statehood would bring about two dramatic tax changes in Puerto Rico. First, the local government would lose $214 million yearly in revenues to accommodate the federal corporate income tax. Second, the corporations in Puerto Rico would be hit by a 267 percent increase in their income taxes, since under the commonwealth formula they paid only $457 million in 1983, whereas under statehood they would have paid $1.7 billion.

The Economic Impact of Statehood on the State Government

Under commonwealth status, the local government has been able to use individual and corporate income taxes as important revenue sources to improve living conditions on the island. The decrease in the infant mortality rate, the increasing educational opportunities for our youth, and the creation of the physical infrastructure needed by industrial firms would not have been possible without these revenues.

Under statehood, however, the local government would be forced to reduce its tax rates on income to accommodate the federal taxes. Statehood would bring a total net loss to the local government of $1.4 billion annually, equivalent to 48 percent of 1983 revenues. This massive loss includes $294 million in federal excise taxes on Puerto Rican rum shipments to the United States and $47 million in federal customs that are now returned to the commonwealth government, $350 million from individual income taxes and $214 million from corporate income taxes, and a $561 million loss in general revenues as a result of the economic recession caused by the plant closings of Section 936 corporations.

Under statehood, the local government would receive the following additional federal funds: $175 million in general revenue sharing, $130 million in Medicaid, $37 million as a social services block grant, $68 million for elementary and secondary education, and $99 million for the Aid to Families with Dependent Children program. Most of these funds are earmarked for specific purposes and clienteles and are much less than the island government's loss in general revenues.

The Cultural Factor

Although the focus of my argument has been the economy, it is undeniable that cultural factors weigh as heavily against statehood for Puerto Rico as the bread-and-butter issues do. We are historically a Spanish-speaking people who cherish our Hispanic culture and would not exchange it for any material benefits. We are, in the words of Pope John Paul II, "located in the midst of Latin American nations."

We are also proud of our linkage with the United States; English is our second language, and we have conscientiously adapted the best democratic institutions of the United States. But we are not willing to relinquish Spanish as our first language nor to change our Hispanic culture for the "American way of life."

Commonwealth status has permitted us to maintain our Hispanic culture while enriching our lives with the English language and the democratic institutions of the United States. No one would gain culturally from changing the status quo—neither the people of Puerto Rico nor the people of the United States, who would be losing a valuable cultural link with the other half of America. PR is the link

we would lose

5
Statehood for Puerto Rico

Carlos Romero Barceló
Former Governor of Puerto Rico
New Progressive Party

All Puerto Ricans are in agreement, regardless of our various political status positions: We are one people—*the people of Puerto Rico*. As such, we have one very basic aspiration: to protect and improve the well-being of our families and of future generations of Puerto Ricans. All of our other aspirations derive from that simple but profoundly important consideration. More than 90 percent of the Puerto Rican people are satisfied and content to be citizens of the United States. We did not ask the United States to take Puerto Rico away from Spain, and we did not ask Congress to make us American citizens in 1917. Nevertheless, the people of Puerto Rico overwhelmingly oppose independence.

The Puerto Rican people can look with pride upon a recent record of truly remarkable achievement in social and economic progress, especially in comparison with our neighbors in the Caribbean and Latin America. That progress could not have come about without, first, the incredible driving force of our people—the desire to give our children more and better opportunities than we have had. It could likewise not have come about without the friendship and cooperation of fellow American citizens from the mainland, nor without the comprehension and financial support of the federal government. Neither could it have come about without the individual liberties and democratic institutions of government that are guaranteed to us by our American citizenship.

Puerto Ricans are increasingly coming to acknowledge the virtues of statehood and the shortcomings of commonwealth, while they continue to recognize, as they always have, that the rhetoric of the independence advocates makes no sense. They recognize the hypocrisy of many spokesmen for independence, as well as the hollow emotionalism of their efforts to appeal to our universal desire to preserve and strengthen our identity as a people. These preachers of separatism denounce the teaching of English in our public schools; they call English a threat to our Puerto Rican culture. The majority of these independence advocates are themselves fluent in English, yet their sense of identity as Puerto Ricans seems not to have been weakened in the slightest. Indeed, they regard themselves as the purest of Puerto Rican patriots. And even more hypocritical are the advocates of "Puerto Rican liberation" who are based in New York and Chicago. The majority of them can barely speak Spanish; others were not even born in Puerto Rico; and still others are not Puerto Ricans, either by birth or heritage, and therefore would probably not even want to live in Puerto Rico if it did become independent!

With the adoption of Puerto Rico's local constitution in 1952, the island underwent a change in nomenclature—from territory to commonwealth. During the governorship of the late Luis Muñoz Marín, many Puerto Ricans accepted his assertion that the events of 1952 had truly produced a kind of autonomy for Puerto Rico. Moreover, they accepted his vision of a "culminated" autonomy, to be attained in the near future, under which Puerto Rico would acquire even greater degrees of self-government, to the point that eventually, our Island might also be described as an "associated republic" of the United States. This concept, combined with the rapid economic progress then being achieved, seemed feasible and attractive, especially as presented by Muñoz, who was a forceful and charismatic leader.

Gradually, however, our people became disillusioned. Over a period of 20 years, Muñoz, and subsequent pro-commonwealth governors, went repeatedly to Congress with proposals for greater autonomy. And they accomplished exactly nothing. During this same period, little by little, we statehooders made the voting public conscious of the truth: that commonwealth status was fundamentally no different from territorial status; that Congress had delegated some of its authority, but that it had surrendered none of its authority. Moreover, as we also pointed out, Congress was constitutionally prohibited from surrendering that authority, except by granting either statehood or independence.

As I have frequently observed in other forums, the "cosmetic autonomy" of the so-called commonwealth compact served the national interest of the United States in 1952, because it permitted Washington, during an era of worldwide decolonization, to have Puerto Rico removed from the United Nations' list of non-self-governing territories. In the years since that objective was achieved, however, Congress and the White House have had no further incentive to delegate additional special privileges to Puerto Rico—especially privileges that have never been enjoyed by any of the states.

In this decade, as difficult economic times have prompted Washington to tighten the federal purse strings, the limitations and weaknesses of commonwealth status have become even more apparent. The most dramatic example occurred when Chairman Robert Dole of the Senate Finance Committee proposed significant changes in Section 936 of the Internal Revenue Code. Commonwealth supporters have always cited Section 936 as one of the greatest advantages of our current political status—the very cornerstone of the highly touted "fiscal autonomy." They have warned that statehood would be economically disastrous, because we would lose all our manufacturing plants after statehood took away their tax exemptions. Statehooders have argued that Congress has every legal right to overturn Section 936, at any time, because no authentic "compact" ever existed between the United States and Puerto Rico.

The U.S. Supreme Court upheld our view in a May 1980 decision, *Harris v. Santiago,* which reaffirmed without comment or discussion—it was a *per curiam* decision—that Puerto Rico falls entirely under the jurisdiction of the Territorial Clause of the federal Constitution, and that Congress can therefore, in the words of the Constitution, "make all needful rules and regulations" with respect to the island. In other words, no bilateral compact has ever really existed between Puerto Rico and the United States.

Two years later, in putting together the package of revenue-raising proposals that eventually became law as the Tax Equity and Fiscal Responsibility Act of 1982, Senator Dole recommended measures that would have dramatically reduced the incentive for mainland companies to operate manufacturing subsidiaries in Puerto Rico. The fiscal autonomy of Puerto Rico was not the product of a bilateral compact; rather, it resulted merely from a section in the Internal Revenue Code that Congress could amend or even repeal. With the invaluable assistance of the White House, sympathetic senators and representatives, influential news media, and many representatives of the private sector, we succeeded after several months in having the Dole proposals amended to reduce the damage they otherwise would have inflicted on our economy.

Commonwealth supporters cannot be justified in opposing statehood on economic grounds. Once we have attained political equality, prosperous Puerto Ricans should pay their share of the federal tax burden; and under statehood, the poor will not bear that burden, just as poor people in the 50 existing states do not pay federal taxes. Some marginal manufacturers may pull out of Puerto Rico when federal corporate taxation arrives, but most will not; and many new firms will begin operating there. An investor views potential profit as a direct function of risk, and the political security and stability offered by statehood will automatically reduce the currently existing demand for a larger return on Puerto Rico investment than is demanded on mainland investment.

As the events of the past three years have made abundantly clear, commonwealth status is predicated not on a compact between peoples, but rather on concessions that Congress has granted and that Congress can take away at any time. It may sound fine, in theory, to propose that Congress draft alternative solutions for Puerto Rico and then submit those resolutions to our people for a vote. And it may sound fine, in theory, to design a blueprint for "friendly independence" and then try to persuade Puerto Ricans to accept it. However, *we in Puerto Rico must be the ones to take the initiative in resolving our political status dilemma.* Outside intervention—be it from the

United Nations, from Washington, from a university campus, or from a "think tank"—cannot and will not be tolerated.

We Puerto Ricans are committed to preserving our identity as a people, and we are committed to preserving our American citizenship. Accordingly, to achieve our goal of social and economic equality with our fellow American citizens, it is our duty to press on with the task of gaining political equality. Full acceptance and full opportunity for Puerto Ricans on the Island and for Puerto Ricans on the mainland will never come about until the people of Puerto Rico demand political equality—and political equality means statehood.

6

Puerto Rico and Independence

The Honorable Rubén Berríos Martínez
Senator, Legislature of Puerto Rico
Puerto Rican Independence Party

The continuation of colonial rule in Puerto Rico is ironically the result, to a large extent, of the United States' image of itself as a
democratic, enlightened, freedom-loving nation. It is true that economic and geopolitical considerations have been key elements that help explain the special attention the United States has paid Puerto Rico. But these
considerations, by themselves, do not suffice to explain the inescapable fact
that 88 years after the American military takeover in 1898, Puerto Rico is
still a possession of the United States.

That the United States continues to foster and maintain Puerto Rico in
the 1980s in a condition of political subservience can only be fully explained
by the incapacity of the United States to recognize the true nature of its role
and to accept the consequences of that role. When the wave of decolonization began to spread after World War II and the founding of the United
Nations, the United States stepped aside and said, in effect, that "all this
talk of colonial powers surely doesn't refer to us." The United States couldn't
conceive of itself as a colonial power and it therefore proceeded to define
away Puerto Rico's colonial condition by saying that Puerto Rico was an
unincorporated territory whose inhabitants were American since 1917 and
who enjoyed substantial home rule.

With this argument, the circle of conscience and convenience was closed,
and the principle of the self-fulfilling prophesy was working at its best. It is
not at all surprising that even today, one still finds support in the United
States for the notion that colonialism by consent is not a bad thing, so long
as the colonial power is the United States.

It should not be difficult to perceive the undertones of racism in all of
this. Isn't there, really, at the root of our problem an unstated premise that
Puerto Ricans can't really administer a republic responsibly, that the American presence provides a "checks and balances" element to the otherwise
"unsteady Latin temperament," that for Puerto Ricans to be wards of the
United States is really for the Puerto Ricans' own good.

But racism also operated in a more subtle and tragic manner. Since
Puerto Ricans were U.S. citizens and they were voting for a continuance of
the status quo, wouldn't support for independence from the United States

be interpreted as a rejection of the Puerto Ricans by their co-citizens from the north? Thus, the fear of being accused of racism served among many influential and well-intentioned sectors of American society (I am thinking of the *New York Times* and the *Washington Post,* for example) as an additional incentive to view the Puerto Rican status quo not as an anachronistic colonial regime but as an "imaginative experiment in American federalism." In the same vein, Puerto Rican school texts and Puerto Rican politicians referred to July 25, 1898, not as the days of American invasion of Puerto Rico but as *el cambio de soberanía*—the change of sovereignty. It was even chosen as the official date to commemorate commonwealth status, that insubstantial and crumbling monument to colonialism by consent.

If Puerto Rico is a colony and if there is a recognition of this basic political fact, then there is no other solution than to proceed forth and dismantle colonialism in Puerto Rico—that is, to design a process by which the United States will renounce its sovereignty over Puerto Rico so that Puerto Rico can organize itself as an independent republic. However, many believed that the United States was "different" in its motives from the European colonial powers. Therefore, the process of decolonization didn't apply to the possessions of the United States. The issue became quite simple: If Puerto Rico was not a colony, the remedy need not be decolonization. In addition, the colonial status quo was reinforced by an even more important consideration: It seemed to be what the Puerto Rican people wanted. Wasn't it true that in free elections, the voters supported the status quo? Wasn't it true that support for independence was quite small?

The issue of whether or not Puerto Ricans want independence is really a red herring—a diversion of attention from the real problem at hand. Independence support in colonial electoral contests is low because of obvious factors, the most important of which is that Puerto Ricans have labored under the justifiable impression created by 88 years of U.S. colonial rule that Puerto Rico would be severely penalized should it opt for independence. The moment U.S. attitude toward independence becomes one of cooperation, we will see its electoral support multiply in Puerto Rico. This is only natural in a relationship in which economic relations have become so intertwined that only a negotiated and carefully designed process toward independence can prevent the economic traumas that would otherwise accompany any attempt to sever relations with the United States in one clean stroke. The long-range interests of the United States and the responsibilities it has incurred after 88 years of colonialism dictate such a course of action for the United States.

The alternatives to moving toward independence are two. The first is to favor the continuing growth of the pro-statehood movement, which developed in Puerto Rico as a result of the contradictions of our colonial condition. This development, which is the direct result of the anti-independence bias of the United States, potentially constitutes a threat to the U.S. federal structure and could create a profound crisis in American political life. If there is a statehood petition in the near future, it will be the beginning of a slippery slope for the U.S. Congress. If the petition is not granted, there will be substantial and dangerous anti-American backlash in Puerto Rico that will fuel the independence movement with feelings of frustration and disenchantment. If the Congress should decide to accept Puerto Rico as a state, the United States will be faced with a combination of the Quebec and Northern Ireland syndromes that will become an open sore for the United States into the foreseeable future and beyond.

The second alternative is the continuation or modification of the status quo. This is, in fact, no alternative at all; internationally, it has lost all credibility, while in Puerto Rico, it has become the structure for the collapse of economic and social vitality. Puerto Rico is rapidly becoming a tropical version of the South Bronx: 30 percent unemployment, 60 percent of the families on food assistance programs, 100,000 drug addicts, sharp decreases in investment as our government is increasingly devoid of even traditional areas of autonomy by encroachment of federal power. The Puerto Rican scene is one of frustration and despair. The status quo is bankrupt—economically, politically, and morally. It only serves to promote the statehood drive and deteriorate the prospects for the future. The commonwealth status quo, in any form or modification, is the problem, not the solution.

It is high time that the United States decided on a policy to make Puerto Rico an independent republic. The United States must be moved toward an institutional realization of its obligations. The growing respect and influence of the Puerto Rican Independence Party (PIP) as a political party in Puerto Rico send a signal to those in positions of power in the United States. Moreover, the PIP has developed an effective international initiative. This initiative has progressively put the U.S. government on the defensive, particularly as traditional friends of the United States continue to cross over to the side of independence. This growing international support for independence is an almost inevitable development, for self-determination is a universally accepted principle; for Puerto Rico, there can be no self-determination until the United States has recognized our independence.

My hope lies in the conviction that sooner or later, enlightened editorial opinion in the United States—conservative and liberal—will apply to Puerto Rico the same standards and values it applies to the world at large; that it will call a colony by its name and demand redress that such condition requires; that it will recognize the existence of Puerto Rico as a nation and will insist on the political realization of nationhood.

The process I foresee and predict will not be an easy one; it is fraught with obstacles and technical difficulties. The process of disengagement will require good will and imagination on the part of both our nations and a willingness to face small but determined pockets of opposition. The alternative, however, can well be a tragedy for both countries.

Part III
Economic Issues

7

Investment and Economic Development in Puerto Rico

José R. Madera Prado
Former Director, Economic Development Administration of Puerto Rico

The First Development Plan

Puerto Rico's first economic development scheme was based on the ideologies of Luis Muñoz Marín and Rexford Guy Tugwell. Both believed, at least in 1942, that our economy had to revolve around agriculture—that land, if equitably distributed and managed, would sustain our growing population. Land reform and attempts to increase agricultural productivity and commercial activities related to agriculture were the first targets of government. Manufacturing was relegated to second place—small-scale industries with local management and capital to satisfy internal demand.

The Puerto Rico Industrial Development Company (PRIDCO), a public corporation, was created in 1942 to establish government factories that would "open the doors to private initiative for new manufacturing activities."

PRIDCO inherited a cement factory established in 1938 by the Puerto Rico Reconstruction Agency and then quickly set up four other basic manufacturing plants. Unfortunately, these efforts did *not* stimulate private industrial investments and, by 1946, PRIDCO could hardly boast of nine factories established under the plan.

Local industries and businesses had always been outside the taxing authority of the federal government since the change in sovereignty in 1898. But in 1921, the Congress decided to grant 100 percent exemption from the corporate federal tax to United States–based parent firm subsidiaries established in any of the possessions and territories of the nation. This policy was embodied in Section 931 of the Internal Revenue Code and was called the Possessions Corporation Law. The intent of the Congress was to stimulate growth and development in its territories and possessions, thus improving the substandard living conditions of American citizens residing outside the continental confines of the mainland states.

At first, Section 931 had little effect in Puerto Rico and in other areas under the U.S. flag. Tax exemption, of course, is only one of the many factors considered by the private sector in making investment and site location decisions. Availability of skilled labor, industrial space, transportation facilities, and built-up infrastructure in general are other factors in the plant location process. Nevertheless, the federal Possessions Corporation Law and Puerto Rico's self-styled industrial incentives law constitute the legal underpinning to the island's development up to the present.

In 1976, the Congress revamped Section 931 to make it more flexible and effective. Section 931 was supplanted by Section 936, which permitted parent firms to repatriate federally exempted profits at will from their Puerto Rican subsidiaries. This obviated the costly and time-consuming repatriation requirements under old Section 931.

I believe we have come to grips with reality and have extrapolated the real meanings implicit in our industrial development of the past four decades. These lessons can be briefly stated as follows:

1. Economic development cannot solely depend on incentives given to manufacturing, ignoring other sectors. Lags in agriculture, services, and so forth, merely cancel industrial progress.

2. Economic development based on industries that depend on low salaries or imported oil is subject to instability and does not fit our realities.

3. Carte blanche tax exemptions institutionalize fiscal inequity at the expense of those already bearing the tax burdens of the whole society.

4. Economic strategies must be revised and adjusted periodically to meet society's growing aspirations and the changing realities of the world.

5. Government subsidies cannot maintain nonviable businesses.

6. Government takeover and operation of private business is generally inefficient and consumes treasury resources that should be devoted to other purposes.

Today's economic focus is based on sensible principles that fit the current world situation and, above all, use what our experience has taught us.

8

General Overview of the Economy of Puerto Rico

Francisco A. Catalá
Associate Professor, University of Puerto Rico
Puerto Rican Independence Party

The Fourth Level Economy

José L. González, a noted Puerto Rican writer living in Mexico, has written an interesting historical interpretation essay, "The Four-Story Country," which—according to my interpretation—has become relevant as a result of the pressing structural imbalance of our economy.

According to González, the first level of Puerto Rico was built upon Afro-Antillean cultural bases that developed during the first three centuries of post-Columbian history. Later, during the last century, two migratory waves arrived to our shores, making up the socioeconomic second level of our island. The first wave was composed of Spanish refugees from the colonies that were fighting for their independence; the second was composed mostly of Corsicans and Catalonians, who staged the colonization of the central regions and became the forging class of the coffee estates.

The principal actors of the last two levels are others. The third level was created after the North American invasion of 1898 and the final expansion of the plantation economy. The fourth level, the one we are living in and also our main topic, is made up of the conjunction of North American capitalism and Puerto Rican populism that emerged during the 1940s.

This fourth level, in which the "modernization" of Puerto Rico has taken place, has been a function of the migration of large segments of the population—more than half a million Puerto Ricans relocated to the United States during the 1950s—and of an industrial policy designed on the model of dependent capitalism. This model is attached basically to two conductive wires. One of them extracts from our country the income on investments, which is the basis of the industrial incentive policy; the other, which is welfare, takes care of the population that has been put aside by the market but has not yet been forced overseas.

The Depletion

Growth of the fourth-level economy has reached the point of stagnation. The real growth of production during the 1982 fiscal year, as stated in government reports, was negative—minus 3.9 percent; expressed in per capita terms, we had a decrease of no less than 4.7 percent. It is foreseen that in fiscal year 1983, the gross product will decrease at least 2.3 percent.

The relative economic stand has persisted since 1973 in spite of the amount of federal funds received. The fixed annual investment in machinery and equipment that makes possible the increase in the productive capacity of the country has remained unchanged during the past decade. From 1981 to 1982, there was, in fact, a reduction of 32 percent in real terms.

The deterioration of the productive activity of the economy, in addition to the population growth, has undermined the standard of living of Puerto Rican families. From 1960 to 1970, the average income per family, expressed in constant prices, increased from $2,539 to $4,013, which amounts to an actual annual increase of 5.8 percent. On the other hand, during the 1970–80 period, this indicator only increased from $4,013 to approximately $4,636, just 1.5 percent annually. During fiscal years 1981 and 1982, the average income per family, in constant dollars, decreased 0.6 and 1.6 percent, respectively.

The depletion of the dynamics of growth has worsened the chronic unemployment of our labor force. For 1973, average unemployment was estimated at 12 percent. For fiscal years 1981 and 1982, that average increased to 20 and 23 percent, respectively. The official unemployment rate for January 1983 was estimated at 25.3 percent. The rate of participation in Puerto Rico—that is, the percentage of the population over 16 included in the labor force—is outstandingly low. In fact, it has been dropping in recent years and reached 40.7 percent in January 1983. This means that official unemployment is an index that underestimates actual unemployment.

In addition, it must be noted that in recent years, the largest increase in employment has occurred in the public sector. From 1979 to the present, both the manufacturing and the trade sectors have reduced their participation in the labor structure.

This scenario leads us to the conclusion that in Puerto Rico, an extreme has been reached in the separation between income and productive work; that is, an ever-growing segment of our population earns income without engaging in productive work.

The most often cited causes for this economic stagnation are diverse. Reagan's "new economy" has been most often blamed. After 1973, the accelerated increase in petroleum prices was faulted. Earlier, during the mid-1960s, at a time when the economy of Puerto Rico was already showing signs of structural weaknesses, several factors were mentioned: the lowering of customs duties because of the Kennedy round negotiations, the high cost of transportation, and the growing impact of the federal minimum wage. These measures impaired Puerto Rico's ability to compete in the U.S. market.

To cope with this situation, the government of Puerto Rico resorted to public indebtedness. From 1971 to 1975, Puerto Rico's public debt increased at an unprecedented rate, ballooning from $1.7 billion to $5.1 billion. By 1982, it had leaped to $8.1 billion. In spite of this policy and the influx of federal funds, the economy of Puerto Rico has not recovered.

The Conductive Wires

As I mentioned earlier, the economy of Puerto Rico is a function of two conductive wires: the dependency wire and the income-extracting wire. The first wire carries the flow of federal funds disbursed in Puerto Rico, including federal grants to the public sector, unilateral payments to individuals, and operational expenses of federal agencies. Dependency should not be equated with welfare, however. Federal disbursements include such earned benefits as pensions, veterans' payments, and social security. However, the bulk of these funds consists of unilateral transfers.

These disbursements increased considerably during the 1970s. In 1969–70, the ratio of net federal disbursements to gross product was 10.4 percent. By 1982, when net federal disbursements climbed to $3.5 billion, the ratio was close to 28 percent.

The productive sector of Puerto Rico feeds the other wire. In 1982, income on investments—profit, dividends, and interest taken out of the economy of Puerto Rico—totaled $4.7 billion. The largest item in this group is income on direct investments, particularly retained earnings of American subsidiaries. Income on investments increased from $593 million in fiscal year 1970 to $4.7 billion in fiscal year 1982. As a ratio of the gross product, it climbed from 12.6 percent to 37.4 percent.

The economy of Puerto Rico has a dependency index of 28 percent, and it pays 37.4 percent of its gross product to foreign businesses as income on investments (which could be redefined as the exploitation index). Its model has been pushed to the limit. The wires are overloaded.

President Reagan's Short-Circuit Policies

President Reagan's "new" economic policy has functioned as a short circuit that affects both conductive wires. It is already directly affecting the dependency wire. The discontinuation of the CETA program and the cuts in the Food Stamps Program are having a great impact on our economy. A relatively marginal effect on the U.S. population becomes a generalized effect in Puerto Rico, where over 50 percent of all families receive assistance from the Food Stamps Program.

It could be argued that the alternative is to reach for the other wire—the wire of income on investments, which is, after all, the backbone of the industrialization program. But, as mentioned earlier, this wire is also overloaded. Besides, it is not insulated from President Reagan's short-circuit policy.

Puerto Rico's appeal to foreign investors is a function of the profit differential with the United States. The manufacturing industry in the United States has an average profit–sales ratio between 5 and 10 percent. In Puerto Rico, as a result of tax exemptions and wage differentials, the ratio exceeds 25 percent. President Reagan's program of accelerated capital depreciation and reduction of corporate taxes tends to reduce this differential, thus diminishing Puerto Rico's appeal as an industrial investment area.

The Fifth Level

The fourth level is crumbling, and it won't be sufficient to shift the furniture to find a solution. It is imperative that we set the foundation for a fifth level. We cannot skip stages; we must start from where we stand. But the new level won't stand firm if Puerto Rico is not the builder of its own home.

The crisis in the two conductive wires of the economy of Puerto Rico—dependency and exploitation—has the aforementioned effect: unemployment and a lowering of the standard of living. It is therefore necessary to start a transcendental effort to remedy the structural imbalance of our economic system. The production base of Puerto Rico must be redesigned to liberate the economy from the dependent capitalism patterns. The flow of federal funds is still a crucial variable in the system, and efforts should be made to define a coherent policy for their use, geared toward production and a reduction of dependency.

Most of the funds received by the public sector have been used for projects that do not correspond to the needs of a reconstruction and economic development program. This has locked us into a vicious circle in which dependency breeds greater dependency. President Reagan's budget cuts show us that a status built on dependency has its foundation in quicksand.

The new style of development must link all sectors of the economy in such a manner that growth in one area does not presume languishing of another. An integration of all sectors and a growing internal financing are imperative. But we must recognize that dependence on external capital, welfare payments, and foreign debt will continue unless a transition to political independence is initiated. Independence can be adequately achieved through an orderly, rational, and responsible transition.

Independence would bring Puerto Rico the authority to establish monetary, trade, wage, and in-migration policies, but it also would end features of its relationship with the United States that have too much economic significance under the actual system. It must be recognized by both parties that various transitional arrangements would be needed to establish a new institutional framework and economic order, consistent with Puerto Rican, North American, and international new requirements.

For instance, recognizing the consequences of suddenly losing federal funds, the Puerto Rican Independence Party (PIP) has proposed that current funding levels be extended temporarily after independence. In lieu of the current forms of aid, however, the PIP has suggested that the federal government contribute to a special development and economic reconstruction fund. This fund would help finance essential government activities until the economy is reoriented and other revenue sources are developed.

Other measures have been proposed to enhance the island's ability to reorient its economic development. Most notably, the PIP has advocated proposals for introducing U.S. tariffs gradually, negotiating the change in currency, and extending credit terms and tax arrangements. Indeed, the Caribbean Basin Initiative, particularly the One-Way Free Trade Proposal, demonstrates the potential for United States–Puerto Rico negotiations toward independence.

The economic crisis should raise our awareness of the flaws of our present economic system and should inspire the search for alternative strategies for development. The two-wire system that characterizes our economy should be replaced with a new fifth level, designed to serve the real needs of our people.

Check
Ch. 9

9

Commonwealth and the Economics of Development

Teodoro Moscoso, Organizer
Hubert C. Barton, Economic Consultant
Economic Development Administration of Puerto Rico

S ince World War II, international economic development strategy has focused on investment. Patterns of investment have varied, depending on the resource mix of different developing countries and on differences in the roles of the government and private sectors in investment decision making. In Puerto Rico, government has actively promoted and subsidized private-sector investment in agriculture, manufacturing, and tourism and has itself invested directly in the essentials of economic infrastructure—notably, education, health, public utilities, and transportation. This is the essence of what has recently been called supply-side economics, but it has been de facto government strategy in Puerto Rico during most of the past four decades. Not all political leaders in San Juan and Washington have recognized the primacy of investment in the development process, nor has there been anything like consensus on who should invest or on how investment can best be maximized and guided into the most productive channels.

In the 1930s, much of the "investment" in Puerto Rico reflected remedial actions taken by the federal government to deal with the ravages of the great depression. The principal agency involved was the Puerto Rico Reconstruction Administration (PRRA). It should be noted that about two-thirds of the federal funds flowing into Puerto Rico today go directly to individuals. An even smaller proportion is invested than had been invested by PRRA half a century ago. Such federal expenditures are of great social benefit, because they flow to low income families and individuals. They have made the pattern of income distribution in Puerto Rico among the most egalitarian in the world. However, their effect on the economy is limited and transitory. In fact, they probably contribute more to the U.S. economy than to the economic development of Puerto Rico.

The financial muscle for the rapid development of the economic infrastructure of the island during the 1940s and early 1950s was provided by an unprecedented revenue windfall. About $160 million in "extra" federal excise taxes on Puerto Rican rum sold in the United States during the World War II whiskey shortage were returned by federal law to the insular treasury.

By 1950, total public debt had risen to $168 million from the very low figure reached at the close of World War II. Debt of the public corporations was $122 million, 73 percent of the total. The corresponding figures for 1983 were total public debt, $8.440 billion, of which the public corporations accounted for $6.276 billion, or 74 percent. Most of this debt was then and is now externally held, and it is clear that the public corporations have been the primary generators of public funds used for economic development financing. Total public debt, which was 23 percent of annual gross domestic product in 1950 is 50 percent today. Debt financing has accelerated economic development and, as evidenced by the ratings of Puerto Rico bond issues, both investment policy and debt management have been generally productive as well as prudent.

The traditional boundaries between the public and private sectors that prevailed before the depression and World War II were no longer sacrosanct. However, administration of some agencies of government, especially in the field of agriculture, became increasingly difficult for lack of clear definition of purpose and functions. As seen by Muñoz, the basic responsibility of the Land Authority was land reform, which had been a principal campaign pledge in his election campaign, whereas Tugwell was more concerned with agricultural development, production of food crops for local consumption, and fostering cooperative enterprises.

The Land Authority was the first of the original nine public corporations to be established, and it had the highest capital appropriations. By 1950, the Land Authority had purchased nearly half the sugar land owned by private corporations in excess of the unenforced federal "500 acre limitation act." About 64,000 acres were put into forty-eight large "proportional benefit" farms, which operated on a profit-sharing system. Puerto Rico has never had an effective agricultural development organization. Government expenditures "on agriculture" have averaged about four times those on manufacturing development, but, for the most part, they have been for rural social programs rather than for agricultural development.

Employment in rural Puerto Rico is now very small—the total in agriculture at about 37,000. Rural population, however, is still in excess of a million people, partly as a result of land reform and the many other social programs intended to improve the quality of life in rural areas. The Land Authority changed the pattern of land ownership and the distribution of agricultural income, but it made little change in the total investment in agriculture—in technology or in total production and income. With Muñoz as president of the Senate and Tugwell as governor, government was being professionalized, but the general political orientation of its leaders was strongly pro-labor, with populist and socialist leanings.

The idea of promoting or attracting private investment in manufacturing and tourism projects was not new, but how to do so effectively and at a reasonable cost had to be worked out. Exemption from corporate income taxes was believed, a priori, to provide the strongest incentive and at a very low cost. However, Governor Tugwell vetoed the tax exemption bill introduced in 1944.

We also had a labor cost advantage compared with the federated states. After a witless application of the Fair Labor Standards Act of 1938, with its 25 cent an hour minimum, had shut down most of the existing apparel industry, Puerto Rico obtained an amendment to the act that enabled special industry committees to recommend minimum wages in Puerto Rico below the federal statutory figure.

As early as the late 1950s, a number of responsible people, including the governor, began to have doubts about the matter of balance in our social and economic progress. Was the economic outpacing the social? Certainly, industrial development was outpacing agriculture. Were local entrepreneurs being displaced by outsiders? Was Puerto Rico's cultural identity being jeopardized by urbanization and massive migration to the U.S. mainland? Should government efforts be concentrated on improving some of the conditions of commonwealth status?

Underlying much of this questioning and criticism was undue faith in the FOMENTO program. It appeared to have become automatic. It was pushing up the economy every year at a rate that would double incomes every decade. There was still widespread poverty, but it was disappearing rapidly. Jobs were waiting in the United States for those who could not find them at home. Average family income had reached $3,000.

We are paying a doubly heavy price for our failure to defend the system of flexible minimum wages, because without this flexible control over labor costs, corporate income tax exemption became meaningless for many manufacturing operations, especially in the low-wage industries. Tax exemption is not an incentive unless a firm earns a profit that would otherwise be taxable. For most manufacturing operations, all important costs except labor costs and property taxes are higher in Puerto Rico than in the United States. It usually takes a labor cost advantage to make a firm profitable in Puerto Rico but, once profitable, it can be doubly so because of exemption from corporate income taxes.

Continuity does not mean that rules should be unchanged but it does mean that whatever changes are made should be in a positive direction. In 1976, we finally negotiated with the U.S. Treasury and the Congress an advance in the attractiveness of our tax exemption program that we had sought since the 1950s. Enactment of Section 936 of the Internal Revenue Code permitted tax-free repatriation of the profits of a subsidiary of a U.S. firm operating in Puerto Rico without liquidating the subsidiary, as had previously been required. A well-meaning Congress, however, insisted that Puerto Rico itself impose a "tollgate" tax on the profits being transferred as compensation for the loss of reinvestment in Puerto Rico that might otherwise take place.

In their efforts to force Puerto Rico to assume a "state-like" posture, statehood advocates have cut our own tax incentives to a point at which existing tax exemption has comparatively little net attraction for many U.S. industrial investors.

The United States is not going to develop the economy of Puerto Rico. Transfer payments to poor families and other federal measures to relieve poverty will continue to apply to Puerto Ricans because we are U.S. citizens. We can continue to benefit from minorities legislation, especially in sales to the military. An "enterprise zone act" would help some regions in the states but would probably add little or nothing to existing investment incentives in Puerto Rico. On the contrary, unless carefully drafted, it could increase the already strong stateside competition for private investment dollars.

We do need help from Washington—the kinds of help that could not be extended to any particular state but that have been and can be provided to us as a commonwealth. We need legislated permanence for Section 936 and "most-favored" tax treatment for U.S. corporate investments in Puerto Rico. Section 936 recognizes the fiscal independence of Puerto Rico. But merely as a matter of equity, it seems to us that if our government is willing to exempt the Section 936 corporations from tax, it is not too much to ask the Treasury of the United States to follow suit. Similarly, to us, it seems only fair and just for the United States to extend at least as favorable corporate tax treatment to firms investing in Puerto Rico as it does to those investing elsewhere in the Caribbean Basin.

The rest is up to us—clarification and simplification of our own rules of the game, a fresh start in agriculture, unified administration of key economic development programs, and an increase by multiples in the promotional efforts of a revitalized and reunified FOMENTO to stimulate investment from all available sources in every creative aspect of our economy and society.

Part IV
International Implications

10
Mainland News Media Coverage of Puerto Rico: Commentary

George McDougall
Former Special Assistant to the Former Governor of Puerto Rico

A fuzzy perception of Puerto Rico's political status pervades much of the national consciousness. In the government, we receive hundreds of letters every year from schoolchildren all across the nation who are doing social studies projects. Sometimes their teachers have them address the Government of Puerto Rico as a foreign country, using overseas postage rates; sometimes they have their pupils include Puerto Rico among the states of the United States of America, using 22-cent stamps on their letters.

We also receive complaints from Puerto Ricans residing on the mainland. Juanita is married to a soldier stationed in South Carolina; she receives checks from her family in Puerto Rico, but the bank on the military base refuses to cash them until they are converted into "American dollars." Or José, who holds a master's degree in finance, is applying for work with the U.S. government's Export-Import Bank in Washington. The personnel officer takes one look at his résumé and says, "Sorry, fella; you were born in Puerto Rico, and we are required to hire only American citizens."

Not only does the general public fail to comprehend "what Puerto Rico is," but there are many instances in which officials of the federal government display total ignorance on this subject. I am sorry to say that the news media are as much to blame as anyone. Examples in recent years are illustrative: The *New York Daily News* publishes weather information from around the world in two categories: "U.S. Cities" and "Foreign Cities." San Juan is listed among the U.S. cities—every day. Nevertheless, on November 26, 1981, a Puerto Rico story in the *Daily News* appeared not under "What Else in the Nation," but under the heading "What Else in the World," a section devoted entirely to *foreign* news.

A *New York Times* editorial in August 1982, devoted entirely to Puerto Rico, said of Puerto Ricans: "No other Americans have so little power to help themselves in Washington." But that same summer, a *New York Times* article by Steven Weisman, datelined Miami, made reference to detention facilities located "in this country and Puerto Rico." And a May 1982 *New York Times* piece, the subject of which was nothing less than a U.S. postage stamp to honor baseball star and humanitarian Roberto Clemente, mentioned that after Clemente's death, "three days of *national* mourning" were proclaimed "in his native Puerto Rico."

The *Wall Street Journal,* on its editorial pages, has repeatedly defended the rights of Puerto Ricans as American citizens and has even expressed sympathy for statehood on several occasions. Over on the news side, though, you can still run across bloopers such as the 1981 headline concerning corporate mischief in Puerto Rico; declared the *Wall Street Journal:* "General Electric Company and Ex-Aides Fined for Bribery *Abroad.*"

United Press International noted that the former Governor of Puerto Rico, Carlos Romero Barceló, is married to an "American"—implying, apparently, that Puerto Ricans are something else. And UPI referred to Haitian refugees landing "in Puerto Rico *or* United States shores"—implying, apparently, that Puerto Rico is not a part of the United States. But UPI also goes in the other direction. A Cuban athlete defected in San Juan, and UPI used the phrase, "Now that he is in America." And in a 1980 pre-election story from San Juan, UPI led with the following: "While other Americans are deciding Tuesday who will be their president, Puerto Ricans will vote in a gubernatorial election."

A *Baltimore Sun* editorial in 1979 referred repeatedly to Puerto Rico as a "country," distinct from the United States, and likewise made clear distinctions between "Americans" and "Puerto Ricans," as different peoples.

Finally, the confusion sometimes becomes downright comical. Back in 1977, when Carlos Romero Barceló was inaugurated for his first term as governor, the headline in the *Greenwood* (South Carolina) *Index-Journal* read: "Puerto Rican President Sworn In."

What does all this mean? On major national and international policy issues, the news media probably do *not* accurately reflect public opinion. But on peripheral issues—issues in which neither the public nor the media take any intense or compelling interest—on these issues the media are more likely to reflect the attitudes of the general public. The public has little knowledge about or interest in Puerto Rico. This combination of ignorance and apathy tends to be reflected in *most* media coverage of Puerto Rico. Data go unverified, stereotypes are reinforced, and reports from on-the-scene correspondents tend to follow safe, predictable patterns, so as not to raise any eyebrows among the editors back home. Why the confusion? Just how *is* Puerto Rico depicted in the media? And *why* is it depicted that way?

Until the 1950s, Puerto Rico's image on the mainland was that of an obscure place where people were terribly poor and where nationalist radicals committed atrocities from time to time. "Image-wise," the island had nowhere to go but up. In 1949, Luis Muñoz Marín became governor and started to turn that image around.

On the one hand, he launched a successful industrialization program, in open and friendly partnership with corporate America. On the other, he exploited to the fullest the visibility he enjoyed both as Puerto Rico's *first* elected governor and as a landslide re-election victor in 1952, 1956, and 1960.

Muñoz was especially well suited to the task of building a favorable public relations posture. He had lived in New York and Washington during much of his youth, and he spoke totally idiomatic English. He had worked as a journalist, and even as a poet, and was extremely articulate as well as extremely astute in dealing with reporters.

By the late 1950s, Luis Muñoz Marín had appeared on the cover of *Time* magazine and had won acclaim throughout the hemisphere as the architect of progress in Puerto Rico, which by then was being heralded as "America's showplace of democracy in the Caribbean." Muñoz had a profound effect on a whole generation of reporters, many of whom have since become editors and columnists. Muñoz was the chief proponent of commonwealth political status, and in my opinion is responsible in large part for the fairly broad support commonwealth status continues to receive in the major news media of our nation. Muñoz was also the Puerto Rican public figure most responsible for promoting the idea that Puerto Rico was not a territory of the United States but rather a "country," "associated" with the United States through a bilateral "compact" between "the peoples" of the island and the mainland.

Luis Muñoz Marín was a man of exceptional talents, and he was in power in Puerto Rico for a very long time. It would be a mistake to underestimate the extent to which he succeeded in inculcating both Puerto Ricans and mainlanders with the concepts he embraced. The same man who could co-opt symbols of the independence movement to broaden support for commonwealth status was also adept at using subtle means to try to prevent the so-called Americanization of Puerto Rico from generating excessive amounts of pro-statehood sentiment, either at home or on the continent.

Those independence symbols, incidentally, were Puerto Rico's flag and anthem. Muñoz adopted a different set of lyrics to the anthem, but its melody had long been identified with the independence movement—and so had the flag. But in 1952, these two emotion-charged items became the official flag and anthem of the Commonwealth, not the Republic, of Puerto Rico.

The editor, columnist, or TV producer who is struggling to make sense out of the Puerto Rico equation must come to grips with the ideological campaigns being waged by Puerto Ricans, and allies of Puerto Rican factions, in the national media. And in this regard, it must be taken into account that most such efforts are directed *against* statehood and also that they can be very sophisticated in tone and content, because Puerto Ricans are extremely sophisticated politically. It is important to remember that Puerto

Rico is an intensely politicized society. In Puerto Rico, it's difficult to agree
even on where to locate a sewer project without the political status question
entering into the debate. A great many of Puerto Rico's journalists have
intense political views of their own. And although they may make an effort
to project a fair amount of objectivity in their local reporting, they may not
always do so.

The media continue to encounter difficulty in deciding whether or not
Puerto Ricans are Americans. Three years ago in the *Wall Street Journal,* I
ran across an anecdote in which a turn-of-the-century Tammany Hall politician, one George Washington Plunkitt, was commenting on Lincoln Steffens's book, *The Shame of the Cities.* The *Journal* quoted politician George
Washington Plunkitt as follows: "Steffens made one good point in his book.
He said he found that Philadelphia, ruled almost entirely by Americans, was
more corrupt than New York, where the Irish do almost all the governin'."
In regard to Puerto Rico's acceptance problem, the message was simply that
these things take time.

11

Press Coverage of Puerto Rico: Response

Juan Manuel García Passalacqua
Columnist, San Juan Star

T he selective inattention of the U.S. press regarding Puerto Rico is not the fault of the U.S. press, when it is precisely the government of Puerto Rico that prints ads of white, upper-class polo players (there is no polo field in Puerto Rico) sipping rum and of happy and well-paid employees in pharmaceutical and other plants exultant over the "excellent conditions" existing on the island. For the American press observer, the happy view is evermore in his own ad pages, while the history of the crisis remains hidden within the confines of the island.

It is only when guerrillas such as the Macheteros blow up eleven planes of the National Guard in San Juan that the crisis becomes evident for the U.S. press, and then only for a few days. Even then, the attention is equally selective; we have seen stories about police corruption in Puerto Rico on the front pages of U.S. papers, but we have not seen any stories about the U.S. government's secret experimental use of tropical forests in Puerto Rico for Vietnam defoliants. The demeaning story for Puerto Rico is printed; the touchy one for the United States is ignored. It is an interesting double standard.

Two crucial factors have been exceptions to the selective inattention rule: presidential politics and international pressures. When a group of Puerto Ricans decided in 1976 to involve the local electorate in U.S. presidential nominations, the issue exploded on the front page of the *New York Times*. When another group of Puerto Ricans decided in 1982 to elevate the issue of Puerto Rico before the United Nations General Assembly, the issue occupied the front page of the *Miami Herald*. The political and international dimensions of the issue, however, receive only sporadic attention—during U.S. nomination campaigns or United Nations sessions. The continuous, careful follow-up of the rapidly deteriorating situation in Puerto Rico remains absent.

The media establishment in the United States has, however, played a crucial policy-oriented role recently in the Puerto Rican situation. It was the *Wall Street Journal* that published the column about then presidential candidate Ronald Reagan's promise to take the initiative to make Puerto Rico the fifty-first state of the Union, as the third leg of his "North American accord" with Canada and Mexico. It was the *New York Times* that, in 1977, first posed the issue of Puerto Rico as "an American dilemma." It was a *Washington Post* editorial that raised the issue of the Reagan administration's change from food stamps to outright checks for Puerto Rican welfare recipients. It was the *Los Angeles Times* that raised the issue in its op-ed page of the Puerto Rican electoral "paralysis" in the 1980 elections. It was CBS News that raised the issue of Puerto Rico's economic dependence on the contributions of U.S. taxpayers. It was NBC News that obtained an on-camera agreement (later rescinded) between Governor Carlos Romero Barceló and opposition leader Rafael Hernández Colón on a yes-or-no referendum on statehood in 1985. It was the *Christian Science Monitor,* the *Washington Post,* the *New York Times,* the *Wall Street Journal,* and the *St. Louis Post Dispatch* that between January 15 and February 3, 1982, questioned the wiseness of President Reagan's statement of that week that he "still" believed statehood was the best solution to the Puerto Rican issue. It was *U.S. News and World Report* that in the 1960s touted Puerto Rico as "the answer to Castro" and in the 1980s called it "a troubled Island." In summary, the reportorial reticence has been more than compensated by an editorial propensity. Why are the U.S. media so prone to evaluate yet so reticent to report?

The media, one understands, will cover only *stories.* In the case of Puerto Rico, however, the U.S. media should understand that the "story" is already happening, that the crisis is real and grave, that the issue is squarely posed before the American Congress and should also be posed before American public opinion. The issue is that the United States has a colony in the Caribbean, that its name is Puerto Rico, that neither violence nor surrender are the solutions for the Puerto Rican people, and that, in the last instance, the situation poses, as Jeffrey Puryear has so brilliantly expounded in this book, a dilemma for the United States. *That* is the Puerto Rican story. It deserves to be covered and to be published by the press in the United States of America.

12
Puerto Rico in an International Context

The Honorable Hernán Padilla
Former Mayor of San Juan

P uerto Rico's relationship with the United States is the political relationship that binds us to the rest of the nation—a relationship that I
believe will eventually be bound even closer together when Puerto
Rico is admitted as the fifty-first state of the Union. I am referring to the
role Puerto Rico can play in the international community—as a partner of
the nation in seeking political and economic progress among our neighbors
in Central America and the Caribbean. And I think there is no better time
to discuss this issue, given the increasing hemispheric and worldwide attention currently being focused on this region and on U.S. policies and actions
in the area.

Puerto Rico's geographical location in the Caribbean, as well as its historical and cultural ties to many nations and peoples of Latin America,
provides the base for its role in the international community. Our island is
the major U.S. presence in the Caribbean and, indeed, in all of Latin America. Puerto Rico is often viewed as a cultural bridge between the United
States and Latin America and the Caribbean. In addition, there are trade
and commercial links between our island and many of its Caribbean neighbors and a great potential for expanding them.

Puerto Rico can play a meaningful role in the Caribbean and other areas
of the hemisphere, particularly in economic areas, because it is the most
economically and technologically advanced area in the region. Our leaders
are willing to share our methods and experiences of economic development
with surrounding regions and peoples. Puerto Rico has undergone a remarkable economic change in the past three decades. Our island emerged
from World War II in economic distress, with its population among the most
impoverished in the hemisphere. But today, within the span of a single generation, Puerto Rico enjoys one of the highest standards of living to be found
anywhere in Latin America and the Caribbean. Our economy, though still
underdeveloped in comparison with that of the nation as a whole, is none-
theless characterized by industrial expansion, an increasingly skilled and di-

versified work force, and a growing middle-class population. These exist in Puerto Rico to a degree unmatched elsewhere in this region.

This stature was accomplished, first, through hard work. Puerto Rico's greatest economic asset is its people. Second, it was achieved through political stability. Although our final political status has yet to be decided, we have proved that a strong and healthy democratic system of government, with free and active participation by all members of society in the political process, creates an environment in which economic and social progress is realized.

Finally, our success in these past three decades is due in large part to our close ties with our fellow U.S. citizens and the functioning of a strong free-enterprise system in Puerto Rico. There can be no doubt that factors such as free trade, the opportunity for individual advancement, and encouragement of the development of a strong private-sector economy have played a vital role in improving our island's standard of living and will continue to do so in the future.

In many ways, Puerto Rico is a remarkably successful example of exactly the type of development—both political and economic—that the United States is seeking to promote in the Caribbean and Central America. The threatening forces within this region, with their false propaganda and active participation in violent revolution, are political and economic failures.

The foreign policy of our nation must clearly demonstrate this fact to the peoples and governments of this region. Both we who serve in positions of leadership, and you, the American press, can find no more successful example of the relationship between democratic government and economic progress than that which exists in Puerto Rico today. We can show that the American political and economic system can work in other areas of Latin America and the Caribbean, because we have shown that it has worked for the people of Puerto Rico.

But I believe that our island has the potential to be more than merely a "showcase" for economic development and political stability in Latin America and the Caribbean. Our role can be more concrete and constructive. Through such initiatives as increased trade and commercial ventures, exchange of technology and technical assistance, and greater interchange of industrial, educational, and cultural resources and institutions, Puerto Rico can contribute toward resolving some of the severe economic and social problems that characterize many of our neighbors in the Caribbean Basin.

Efforts by Cuba and other pro-Soviet governments to have the case of Puerto Rico brought to the General Assembly of the United Nations have not been successful. Indeed, as part of the U.S. delegation to the U.N. General Assembly, I participated in efforts to defeat a resolution introduced by Cuba on this very issue. I am convinced that the international community believes, as we believe, that the present commonwealth status is transitory and inadequate and that there is need for a revision of the relationship between the United States and Puerto Rico. Yet the United Nations acted properly when the General Assembly sustained our view that the solution of the status problem is the sole responsibility of the people of Puerto Rico and the United States, without outside interference of the international community.

Nevertheless, we must recognize that Puerto Rico's political status presents a nagging issue for the United States in the international community. How can we urge other countries and governments to establish political systems based on the full and active participation of their peoples in democratic processes when a group of U.S. citizens cannot fully do so?

This issue will be fully resolved when Puerto Rico becomes a state of the Union, as I am convinced it will. In the meantime, however, Puerto Rico's potential for increased involvement in the region is very real. Through this involvement, we can demonstrate to other peoples of the Caribbean Basin the role America desires to play in this region—to work toward political stability and economic prosperity, not through civil war and armed revolution but through democratic government and economic enterprise. In this way, the relationship between Puerto Rico and the nation is strengthened, as is the relationship between the United States and the Caribbean Basin.

For ourselves, the goal of Puerto Rico is to seek political and economic equality within a framework that will bring about a higher quality of life for our citizens. At the same time, the process through which this is accomplished should be an illustration to the rest of the hemisphere, and to the world, of the advantages of America's political and economic systems.

Puerto Rico is becoming more aware of its role and presence in the international community. We are a potential gateway between very diverse regions of the Western hemisphere, between conflicting political and economic systems, between viable and important marketplaces, and even between different cultures and lifestyles.

Puerto Ricans are willing, able, and qualified to join the nation's efforts to improve international relations and bring about a profound understanding of our neighbors' needs and aspirations. I encourage the national press to focus more attention and debate on this important aspect of Puerto Rico's relationship with the United States.

13

Puerto Rico and the Caribbean Basin Initiative

Stephen Lande
Vice-President, Manchester Associates

Because of the deeply rooted and special relationship between the mainland and Puerto Rico, a successful Caribbean Basin Initiative (CBI) must involve measures of direct benefit to the island. As Ambassador William Brock, former U.S. Trade Representative, stated, we would be "shooting ourselves in the foot" if legislation did not take Puerto Rico's interests into account.

It is clear that a prosperous Caribbean will be to the advantage of Puerto Rico. Given the different wage rates and skill levels, it was felt by those drawing up the CBI that there were more opportunities for complementary and cooperative ventures than for divisive competition between Puerto Rico and the other beneficiaries. With this in mind, the CBI provides both a market opening for Caribbean imports into the United States and special rules to encourage Puerto Rican and Caribbean cooperation, similar to the so-called *maquiladora* program.

Under the concept of "twinning," which has been advanced by Puerto Rico and Jamaica, there is a division of labor between production centers. The more labor-intensive activities are carried out by the CBI countries, and the other, "higher-tech" aspects of the operation are carried out in Puerto Rico.

The initial CBI also provided for measures designed to provide benefits for Puerto Rico that had no direct bearing on the Caribbean. To the extent that benefits were being extended to the Caribbean that were already available to Puerto Rico in the tax area, it was only appropriate to expand Puerto Rico's benefits in this area. Puerto Rico has been disadvantaged by the investment-promotion tax reductions in the 1981 tax act. They offset some of the advantages offered to Puerto Rico in its tax-exempt status for multinationals located on the island. The CBI proposal therefore included a mechanism by which firms in Puerto Rico could share in the accelerated depreciation and leasing provisions of the act.

In addition, steps were taken to assure that Puerto Rico would not be hurt by an increase in Caribbean rum exports. A large part of the Puerto

Rican budget is derived from excise taxes collected on sales of its rum in the United States. Under the CBI proposal, Puerto Rico and the Virgin Islands would also receive excise taxes collected on the sale of Jamaican and other Caribbean rum in the United States. Funds were set aside, at no expense to the other beneficiary nations, to compensate for any potential lost tax revenue for Puerto Rico.

The Congress has stripped away some of the basic provisions of the Caribbean Basin Initiative, including many of the specific advantages set aside for Puerto Rico. The strength of protectionism was greater than had been anticipated, with the result that some products of direct interest to the Caribbean were removed from the list of those eligible for duty-free entry into the U.S. market. In addition to the textile exclusions in the original proposal, Congress excluded important products to the Caribbean, such as footwear, other leather products, and tuna fish. Similarly, the very carefully conceived group of investment incentives centering on the 10 percent investment tax credit were also eliminated from the program.

Much depends on the success of Puerto Rico in expanding its links with the Caribbean. This, in turn, depends on the ability of Puerto Rico to make the twinning concept work. To encourage this, the CBI contains specific provisions that will make it more advantageous for Puerto Rico and the Caribbean to engage in joint manufacturing than for similar operations involving the mainland and the Caribbean. Under the CBI's rule-of-origin provisions, there must be a minimum of 20 percent Caribbean input for a product to be eligible for duty-free treatment if the product has 15 percent or more mainland input. However, there is no required minimum Caribbean input if there is a minimum of 35 percent Puerto Rican input.

The second possible area for cooperation is between Puerto Rico and Central America. For too long, the common Spanish heritage and language of these areas have been overlooked. Political stability will return someday to Central America. Links have already been established with more stable areas, such as Panama. Puerto Rico has a unique opportunity to expand economic cooperation and prosperity.

The third area relies on Puerto Rico's potential as a service and financial center for the region. Puerto Rico is becoming a major banking community, providing links to Florida and New York. Here again, the location of Puerto Rico can be most helpful in assuring that the necessary information flows that are such an important component of current development strategy result in increased Puerto Rican service activity in the other Caribbean countries. For example, Puerto Rico is a rich reserve of Section 936 funds, and it certainly is the hope of other Caribbean countries—particularly the Dominican Republic—that Puerto Rico and the Congress would agree that among the permissible uses of these funds will be the investment of a small part of them in development projects in the Caribbean countries.

The fourth and perhaps most overlooked area of importance is the fact that Puerto Rico's development experiment offers many valuable lessons to its Caribbean neighbors. The great strides made by the island were admired throughout the region, and other nations wish to emulate the success of Operation Bootstrap. Like any other area that is more successful than its neighbors, Puerto Rico must be careful not to impose its views. Nevertheless, Puerto Rico's successful experiences in health care, education, sanitation, and so forth, offer the possibility of cooperation between Puerto Rico and its neighbors.

Long-term benefits to Puerto Rico in developing links with its Caribbean neighbors are substantial, and they should not be forgone for shortsighted reasons. Similarly, the Caribbean experience will be enriched and enhanced by its links with Puerto Rico.

Part V
Overlap with Mainland Economics

14
Analysis of the U.S. Treasury Proposal to Rebuild Section 936 of the Internal Revenue Code

Antonio J. Colorado Laguna
Director, Economic Development Administration
of Puerto Rico

Introduction

On November 27, 1984, the U.S. Department of the Treasury submitted to the president a report on tax simplification and tax reform, recommending a variety of changes in the Internal Revenue Code.[1] Key objectives are to obtain revenues from previously untaxed sources so that general tax rates may be reduced, to eliminate unwarranted tax incentives for particular kinds of investments, and to encourage continued economic growth.

One measure proposed by the Treasury Department is the repeal of Section 936. The Treasury plan would replace Section 936 with a temporary scheme of limited tax credits, based on a diminishing percentage of the federal minimum wage and culminating in the complete elimination of any tax preference for Puerto Rico. Such action not only would devastate the economy of Puerto Rico but also would cause severe harm to important domestic and foreign policy interests of the United States—without advancing the basic objectives of the tax reform plan.

If Section 936 were repealed, unemployment in Puerto Rico would climb within 7 years from its already high level of 20 percent to nearly 30 percent.[2] Real industrial net output over the 5-year period following repeal would drop by a cumulative amount of approximately $14.5 billion.[3] Many corporations currently operating under Section 936 ("possessions corporations") would relocate in foreign countries; the flight of those corporations—and the uncertainty created by the repeal of Section 936 as to the heretofore unquestioned commitment of the United States to Puerto Rico's economic viability—would materially damage the credit-worthiness of the commonwealth and would impair the ratings of commonwealth debt obligations.[4] The withdrawal and nonreplenishment of Section 936 funds—now more than 43 percent of total commercial bank deposits in Puerto Rico[5]—could lead to bank failures, which would have to be covered by insurance payments from the federal treasury. At a minimum, the withdrawal of funds would severely limit the lending capacity of these institutions, further damaging Puerto Rico's prospect for economic development.

These adverse effects on Puerto Rico's economy would trigger dramatically increased migration by residents of Puerto Rico to the mainland, creating serious new problems in already troubled areas.[6] Because applicable benefit levels under entitlement programs are higher for residents of the mainland, such migration would cause substantially increased federal transfer payments, even with no new programs to meet the special needs of those involved.

Major foreign policy problems would also result. The destabilization of Puerto Rico would undermine its strategic value for the United States in the Caribbean. The base agreement between the United States and Panama will expire in the year 2000. The only other major U.S. naval base in this important region is in Cuba. New creative initiatives by Puerto Rico to use Section 936 funds for investments in Puerto Rico that will promote twin-plant projects[7]—involving new flows of private capital into countries that are beneficiaries of the Caribbean Basin Initiative (CBI)—would be aborted. All this would result in considerable and lasting harm to the foreign policy and national security interests of the United States throughout Latin America.

The Need for the Section 936 Incentive

Incentives for Enterprise

President Reagan has recognized, in his enterprise zone proposal, the compelling nature of the need to substitute enterprise for dependency in areas of pervasive poverty and unemployment. In the budget proposals for fiscal year 1986, the Reagan administration renewed its request for enterprise zone legislation.[8] The centerpiece of this legislation is a package of tax credits and other tax incentives to stimulate economic development in those depressed areas.[9]

The Puerto Rican Economy

Unemployment in Puerto Rico is 20 percent—approximately three times the mainland average. In 1984, per capita income in Puerto Rico was less than one-third the mainland figure—$4,096 compared with $12,858. In 1982, per capita income of people living in each of the three poorest states was more than double that of people living in Puerto Rico. In 1980, the percentage of people living below the federal poverty level was more than five times greater in Puerto Rico than on the mainland.

Despite pressing problems, federal transfer payments to individuals in Puerto Rico on a per capita basis were, as of 1982, only about two-thirds of the national average.[10] Moreover, such payments have been significantly reduced, and Puerto Rico has suffered a greater per capita decline than all but three states.

Rafael Hernández Colón emphasized in his inaugural address on January 2, 1985, that his administration would be "committed to improving the quality of life in [Puerto Rico] through the work and efforts of all Puerto Ricans." The governor stressed: "These people do not want to be a burden to the Federal Government or to anyone." Puerto Rico is actively involved in the continuing development of strategies for promoting economic self-sufficiency.

Effectiveness of the Section 936 Incentive

The Treasury Department's Fourth Report does not deny the compelling need for an incentive to attract enterprise to Puerto Rico. To the contrary, the report makes the following categorical finding:

> The reduced competitiveness of Puerto Rican labor and the fall in U.S. tariffs on imports from competing developing countries decreased the non-tax incentives for locating in Puerto Rico. *Exemption from U.S. and Puerto Rican taxation is therefore a principal factor attracting firms to the Commonwealth.*[11]

The Tax Reform Report concludes, nevertheless, that Section 936 has not fulfilled its purpose, largely because unemployment has remained relatively high.[12] This conclusion is erroneous. Had it not been for Section 936, unemployment in Puerto Rico would have been much higher. The incentive provided by Section 936 has prevented employment losses, has enhanced the quality of Puerto Rican jobs, and in all respects has generated benefits that far exceed any costs.

The Tax Reform Report's conclusion that Section 936 has been ineffective because the rate of unemployment in Puerto Rico has not significantly decreased during the past decade neglects the significance of the multiple determinants of employment levels in Puerto Rico. In recent years, Section 936 has indeed prevented or mitigated major employment losses.

Ninety-nine percent of Puerto Rico's electrical energy needs are met by petroleum;[13] in contrast, only 6.5 percent of electrical energy needs on the mainland are met by petroleum.[14] The worldwide petroleum price increases of the 1970s dramatically raised the cost of energy on the island, adding to the already high cost of maintaining manufacturing operations there.[15] The oil shocks also virtually destroyed Puerto Rico's petrochemical industry, which had relied on the projected availability of less expensive oil and of sufficient mainland markets for its downstream products.[16]

Manufacturing costs in Puerto Rico have also climbed in recent years as a result of sharp increases in wages. In some industries, such as chemicals, average hourly earnings increased by nearly 750 percent from 1955 to 1980, nearly double the rate of increase on the mainland.[17] Such wage increases have been caused, in significant part, by the imposition on Puerto Rico of the minimum-wage requirements of the Fair Labor Standards Act. Reductions in U.S. tariff levels have enabled low-wage foreign competitors to take traditional United States markets away from Puerto Rico. The average level of the tariff protection has declined by nearly 60 percent since 1960.[18]

Puerto Rican companies are further disadvantaged vis-à-vis foreign competitors by the Jones Act,[19] which requires that they transport raw materials and finished goods between Puerto Rico and the mainland on U.S. bottoms, whereas foreign competitors can make use of much less costly foreign ships. In certain industries, these forces have led to substantial employment loss.

Effects

If Section 936 were repealed, the incentive for reincorporation created by deferral and the foreign tax credit would strongly favor foreign countries over Puerto Rico for new investments. In the absence of Section 936, the attractiveness of low foreign wage rates and the freedom from U.S. regulations would be likely to attract many labor-intensive operations to such low-wage foreign sites.

Conclusion

Repeal of Section 936 would not further the key objectives of the president's tax reform commitment. It would not increase federal tax revenues to permit a more equitable sharing of the tax burden. On the contrary, such a repeal would almost certainly add significantly to the federal deficit at a time when additions to the federal deficit should be limited to only the most compelling circumstances. Repeal of Section 936 would surely entail adverse consequences for U.S. national security interests as well as for the federal deficit and the future of Puerto Rico. An objective assessment of these consequences reveals a compelling case for the preservation and stability of Section 936, not its demise.

Section 936 has worked well to sustain and qualitatively improve employment in Puerto Rico and to showcase in the impoverished Caribbean the economic miracle that American free enterprise can effect.

Notes

1. U.S. Department of the Treasury, *Tax Reform for Fairness, Simplicity and Economic Growth: Treasury Department Report to the President* (Washington, D.C.: Government Printing Office, 1984; hereafter, *Tax Reform Report*).

2. See T. Lane, "The Impact on the Puerto Rican Economy of Repealing Section 936," chapter 15 of this volume. Although the Lane study assumes an effective date of repeal different from that in the Treasury proposal, the effect after the specified interval would be the same.

3. Ibid.

4. Smith Barney, Harris Upham and Co., *Puerto Rico: An Update on Debt Security: the Consequences of the Treasury Proposal to Repeal Section 936.* (March 1985), pp. 2, 6.

5. H. Calero, "Understanding the Economic Recovery: Some Open Issues," *Puerto Rico Business Review* (April 1984): 16.

6. Puerto Ricans are citizens of the United States, and they are free to migrate to the mainland. See 8 U.S.C. 1402. In 1980, the resident population of Puerto Rico was 3.2 million; an additional 2 million Puerto Ricans resided on the mainland. Bureau of the Census, *Statistical Abstract of the United States* (Washington, D.C.: Government Printing Office, 1984), pp. 40, 844.

7. Twin-plant projects generally involve arrangements by a corporation operating in Puerto Rico for the manufacture of components in a neighboring country, either through contract manufacturing or establishment of a subsidiary.

8. See Office of Management and Budget, *Budget of the United States Government for Fiscal Year 1986* (Washington, D.C.: Government Printing Office, 1985), pp. 4–9.

9. Ibid.

10. For purposes of transfer payments, some federal programs treat Puerto Rico as a state, whereas others impose a ceiling on payments to Puerto Rico or exclude Puerto Rico altogether.

11. U.S. Department of the Treasury, *The Operation and Effect of the Possessions Corporation System of Taxation,* Fourth Report (Washington, D.C.: Government Printing Office, February 1983; hereafter, Fourth Report), p. 56 (emphasis added). This report is the most recent annual report on Section 936 available to date.

12. See *Tax Reform Report,* Vol. 2, p. 308.

13. Puerto Rico Electronic Power Authority, Office of Power Revenue Bands, Series I, *Official Statement 14* (March 8, 1984).

14. Bureau of the Census, *Statistical Abstract of the United States,* pp. 581, 583. United States data are for 1982.

15. Major shocks occurred in 1973, when the price of crude oil jumped by 75 percent, and in 1979, when the price increased by 71 percent. Ibid., p. 578.

16. Puerto Rico Planning Board, *Informe Economico al Gobernador* (San Juan: Commonwealth of Puerto Rico, 1983).

17. Fourth Report, p. 44.

18. Bureau of the Census. *Statistical Abstract of the United States.*

19. 39 Stat. 951 (1917), as amended by Public Law No. 600, 64 Stat. 314 (1950).

15
The Impact of Repealing Section 936 on the Puerto Rican Economy

Theodore Lane
Office of Economic Research,
Economic Development Administration
of Puerto Rico

Introduction

To estimate the impact on Puerto Rico of repealing the U.S. Tax Code's Section 936, the island's economy and future performance was simulated. The major projection underlying the forecast was the U.S. Department of Labor, Bureau of Labor Statistics, 1990 projection of employment by industry for the U.S. economy. We assumed that each manufacturing industry would grow at the same rate in Puerto Rico as it did on the mainland. The Section 936 repeal forecast was based on the following assumptions:

The Food Products manufacturing industry is tied to Puerto Rico's natural resources and would be uneffected by 936's repeal. Otherwise:

Manufacturing industries with small average firm investment (under $1 million in assets), which produce mostly for local and regional markets, would be unaffected by 936's repeal.

Manufacturing industries with moderate average firm investment ($1 to $5 million in assets) would begin relocating immediately, and output would fall at a rate of 10 percent per year between 1985 and 1990.

Manufacturing industries with high average firm investment (over $5 million in assets) would not begin relocating until 1988, after which output would decline at a rate of 12.5 percent per year until 1990.

Reductions in plant expansions and replacement of existing capacity would cause output and employment levels in the construction industry to remain at their 1983 levels.

Findings

If Section 936 remains in place, real industrial net income in Puerto Rico is expected to grow at a moderate compound annual rate of 1.97 percent, increasing from $14.7 billion in 1983 to $16.8 billion in 1990. If Section 936 is repealed, Puerto Rico's real industrial net income is expected to fall by about 2 percent annually, reaching a level of $12.8 billion by 1990 (in 1983 purchasing value). Over the 5-year period 1986–90, the repeal of Section 936 would cause a cumulative loss of about $14.5 billion in real industrial output (income). Puerto Rico's real industrial net income in 1990, if Section 936 is repealed, would fall to its lowest level since 1977.

If Section 936 remains in place, total employment in Puerto Rico is expected to grow at a moderate to slow rate of 1.66 percent per year, reaching a level of 819,000 jobs by 1990. If Section 936 is repealed, total employment would fall at an average annual rate of −1.24 percent, to a 1990 level of 650,000 jobs in 1990. The net job loss between 1985 and 1990 resulting from repeal of Section 936 would be about 169,000 jobs. Total employment in Puerto Rico would fall to its lowest level since 1970.

If Section 936 is left in place, unemployment in Puerto Rico is expected to fall from its 1982 rate of 21.7 percent to a rate of 16.7 percent in 1990. If Section 936 is repealed, the unemployment rate would rise to 33.5 percent in 1990, the highest rate since Operation Bootstrap began 45 years ago.

It is doubtful that observed unemployment in Puerto Rico will ever reach 33.5 percent. Recent research findings strongly indicate that Puerto Ricans have a positive preference to remain at home but are pushed onto the mainland when real economic growth doesn't keep up with natural population increases. Since 1975, the unemployment rate, which appears to trigger out-migration, has been in the range of 18 to 20 percent. Using the 20 percent rate as an out-migration trigger and applying it to the 1990 economic projection yields an estimate of between 475,000 and 500,000 *additional* migrants from Puerto Rico to the mainland.

Conclusions

The repeal of Section 936 would be disastrous for Puerto Rico's economy. By 1990, repeal would have (1) cost Puerto Rico over $14.5 billion in reduced industrial income and output; (2) caused the net loss of more than 165,000 jobs; and (3) raised unemployment to over 30 percent or, alternatively, caused an additional half-million Puerto Ricans to migrate from the island to the mainland.

Overall, the repeal of Section 936 would wipe out the last two decades of economic programs in Puerto Rico and would return the island to levels of material welfare not seen since the early days of Operation Bootstrap. Effectively, it would plunge Puerto Rico back into the lowest tier of the world's developing regions.

Part VI
Overlap with Mainland Politics

16
The Importance of Puerto Rico in National Politics: Commentary

The Honorable Maurice A. Ferre
Former Mayor of Miami

Whether *de juris* or *de facto,* Puerto Rico remains a colony. The tragedy of Puerto Rico is that, although Puerto Ricans are individually free and have improved the material quality of their lives since they were given United States citizenship, Puerto Rican dignity has not been sufficiently realized. Therefore, the pursuit of happiness of Puerto Ricans is found wanting by most.

Happiness cannot be achieved without dignity, and dignity cannot exist so long as the political status of Puerto Rico remains in limbo. Improving the quality of life does not solve the basic problem. Either Puerto Rico must have its independence or it must be allowed to join the mainstream of the American system as a state.

Although I believe that the most honorable conclusion to the status dilemma is independence, I also believe that for practical and patriotic reasons, statehood is the only viable conclusion of our political status problem. It will indeed ensure dignity to the people of Puerto Rico. The incorporation of Puerto Rico as a state would be an entry to the Union of a different culture and language. Unlike New Mexico and Hawaii, however, Puerto Rico could maintain its culture, although special conditions for incorporation as a state would be required.

The United States must accept that the integration of Puerto Rico into the mainstream does not require amalgamation. Integration without amalgamation would be the most severe test of the Sixteenth Amendment to the Constitution. Equal rights under the law speak to life and liberty, but also to the pursuit of happiness.

The conclusion of this American dilemma, by granting Puerto Rico either independence or statehood, will have a great impact on the relations between the United States and Latin America and between the United States and the Third World. It will also affect the solution to our internal problems in our own "third world"—the 40 million people who live within the United States but because of poverty, lack of opportunity and education, and discrimination have not enjoyed the full blessings of our country.

It is time for Washington, the American nation, and the people of Puerto Rico to face this important issue and begin to solve jointly the missing link in Puerto Rico's recent history—its dignity and our dignity as Americans so long as the United States remains a colonial metropolis.

17

Puerto Rico's Impact on the U.S. Congress: Commentary

The Honorable Robert Garcia
U.S. Congressman

Politics in Puerto Rico is not an avocation; it is a passion. Voting is more than a civic responsibility; it is a statement of belief, a symbol of this passion. The U.S. association with Puerto Rico began with the war of 1898. The prize in the Spanish-American War was not Puerto Rico; it was Cuba and the Philippines. Yet it is Puerto Rico that has remained intimately associated with the United States.

In discussing Puerto Rico, it's important to have an understanding of the history of its relationship with the United States. For 400 years, prior to the war of 1898, Puerto Rico was a half-forgotten possession of the Spanish Empire. The latter part of the nineteenth century saw Spain's tarnished glory fade into oblivion with the onslaught of its war with the United States.

That war was ostensibly to help Cuban patriots in their struggle for independence from Spain. Cuba became independent with the Teller Amendment of 1898. The Foraker Act of 1900 made Puerto Rico an unicorporated territory, and provided it with a resident commissioner to the United States. By 1902, the commissioner was admitted to the floor of the House; by 1904, he was afforded all the rights of delegates from other incorporated territories.

In 1917, with the passage of the Jones Act, Puerto Ricans received U.S. citizenship, significantly changing the relationship of the island with the mainland. Still, it wasn't until the Crawford-Butler Act was passed in 1947 that Puerto Ricans were allowed to elect their own governor.

Puerto Rico became an *estadio libre asociado,* or commonwealth, in 1952, when it adopted a constitution. Since that time, it has had its own internal government and has produced a remarkable array of effective leaders. The people of Puerto Rico have always appreciated and understood the responsibility involved in maintaining a democracy. This leads me to believe that the only acceptable solution to the question of status is for the people of that island to decide their own fate.

The voting rate in Puerto Rico is about 80 percent. The people care, passionately, about their fate—whether it be statehood, commonwealth, or independence. Puerto Rico is blessed with a sophisticated electorate. Those who favor terrorism as a means for deciding the future of Puerto Rico are a tiny minority. They have not been successful in their efforts because the Puerto Rican people will not tolerate terrorism as a means of political expression. The ballot is the accepted way of determining the island's politics.

The last four U.S. presidents have come out in favor of statehood. Yet despite their good intentions, they did not really help the Puerto Rican people decide what was best for them. What should be done is for the federal government to encourage the three primary groups within Puerto Rican politics to come up with comprehensive proposals for their positions and present them to Congress and the executive branch so that these positions are more thoroughly understood. This should precede a plebiscite held by the Puerto Rican people on these options. This kind of encouragement would be helpful in that it would let the people of the island know that the federal government understands and accepts the fact that they can decide their own fate.

But perhaps more importantly for the immediate future, the Congress and executive branch could step up assistance to Puerto Rico, helping the Puerto Ricans to build their economy. We could also do this by encouraging the growth of the island's business community. Puerto Rico offers an incredible market for mainland goods. It can only help business on the mainland if the Puerto Rican economy continues to grow.

Both of my parents were born in Puerto Rico; consequently, my spiritual ties to the island are very strong. I believe in the character and integrity of the Puerto Rican people, and I'm certain that these characteristics will enable them to make the right decision about their future. When we must do, however, is stop treating Puerto Rico like a forgotten stepchild and realize that the people of Puerto Rico are quite capable of deciding their own fate.

18

The Reluctant Dancing Partner: Washington Power Politics and the Puerto Rican Malaise

Anne Nelson
Journalist

P eople were telling me to start watching Puerto Rico years ago," a young State Department officer for an explosive Central American country commented recently. "They were saying that within a few years the revolutionary forces could really take off."

This may have been a reasonable prediction in 1950, with some faint echoes as late as 1975. But as the 1984 elections approached, Puerto Ricans showed more fear than enthusiasm for violent change. One reason is that the island's advantage over the rest of Latin America has never been more apparent, especially in its unique access to the mainland's federal treasury. In 1980, federal assistance accounted for 29 percent of the island's gross domestic product, and 60 percent of its residents were on food stamps. This beneficence stands in sharp contrast to the situation brought about by the Latin American debt crisis and to the pressure international bankers and the IMF are exerting on the fragile democracies of Argentina and Mexico.

Puerto Rico is in the midst of an institutional crisis. For the first time, the greatest enemy of the commonwealth system is neither the independence movement nor the statehood movement but rather the decaying institutions of commonwealth itself. Ever since Puerto Rico became a U.S. possession in 1898, its leaders have been engaged in a complex minuet with the powers that be in Washington, defining and redefining their status in the effort to gain a less lopsided partnership. The pages of legislation, litigation, and executive orders have multiplied, but in every real sense, Puerto Rico's powers of self-government have declined since the commonwealth was established in 1952. If anything, that decline has accelerated over the last decade.

Because the United States established its presence in Puerto Rico so early and so completely, U.S. attitudes toward the island can serve as indicators for future policies toward the rest of Latin America. In 1898, invading General Nelson Miles told the Puerto Ricans: "We have not come to make war against a people of a country that for centuries has been oppressed, but on the contrary, to bring you protection . . . and to bestow upon you the immunities and blessings of the liberal institutions of our government."

In Puerto Rico, the contradiction reached a critical point with World War II: the territorial assimilation was complete, with a conspicuous U.S. military presence, but the "blessings of the liberal institutions" were all but invisible. Power was exercised from Washington on a one-way basis. Governors of the island were political appointees who, in the words of one of them, "went there from the United States with no previous experience whatsoever, speaking not a word of Spanish." The lack of a clear-cut status was more than a mere identity crisis; it was an administrative disaster. Foreign countries could find leverage at the Department of State and within the rules of international diplomacy. The forty-eight states relied on their legislators to pork-barrel and logroll concessions from each other, the administration, and the bureaucracy. But Puerto Rico fell in the cracks, administered first by the Department of War and then transferred to the Department of the Interior in 1934. The politicians of Puerto Rico who chose to seek power in Washington were left to make half-hearted gestures toward statehood or independence as their only expression of dissatisfaction, knowing at the same time that the power to grant a change in status lay exclusively with the U.S. Congress. The impasse was broken only by the coincidence of three remarkable figures—Luis Muñoz Marín, Rexford Tugwell, and Franklin Delano Roosevelt—in their respective political arenas.

Muñoz, the Commonwealth, and the New Deal

Muñoz's achievement was very much a product of its times and circumstances. Muñoz had been reluctant to sacrifice his *independentista* vision until he saw the devastating poverty of the island sharpened by Hurricane San Felipe and the Depression.

There was a convenient coincidence of style, social philosophy, and political method between Muñoz and the New Dealers. Washington was going through a stage of enormously strengthening the executive branch and enlarging the domain of the federal government, to the detriment of states' rights and congressional powers. Muñoz applied his considerable charisma to his lobbying efforts in Washington, with as much vigor as he had exhibited in his populist campaigns in the Puerto Rican countryside. It was an alliance of conviction as well as necessity; Muñoz quibbled with the New Dealers in Washington often and angrily, but his Popular Democratic Party (PPD) was as faithful in spirit to Roosevelt's cadre of Democrats as any state-level party organization on the mainland.

But Muñoz and his party assimilated many of the weaknesses of the New Deal Democratic alliance as well. Their social reforms depended on federal funds, which themselves depended on the largesse of Congress. The PPD's political message, *"Pan, tierra y libertad,"* pointed toward the creation of a new, reformed peasant class, cushioned against the ravages of rural poverty. But the PPD's economic message of industrialization and emigration was bound to do away with the peasant class as well as the poverty. After decades of economic transformation, the PPD, like the mainland Democrats in the 1980s, found that successful application of their programs had the effect of eradicating their strongest constituencies; after a few decades, the *jíbaro* in his *pava* who voted *popular* would go to New York, move back to a factory job in San Juan, and start voting *republicano*.

Muñoz's legacy of commonwealth status outlasted both his own rule and the hegemony of the Popular Democratic Party. At the time of its creation, the commonwealth was viewed as a variation of the British dominion status of Canada or New Zealand. The discrepancies of power within the commonwealth's compact with the United States, on the other hand, were never resolved. Instead, they steadily worsened with the inevitable divergences of needs and ideologies between the administrations in Washington and San Juan—to the disappointment of the commonwealth's original architects. When these areas were belatedly defined, it was generally to further limit, rather than expand, Puerto Rican powers of self-government.

Muñoz and his lieutenants enjoyed unprecedented levels of prestige. But it was prestige that was reflected within the context of Latin America, not the United States. Puerto Ricans were named head of the Alliance for Progress and deputy assistant secretary of state for Latin America, but this did nothing to further Puerto Rican goals in the U.S. Congress. The one institutional change brought about under Kennedy was to move Puerto Rico's affairs outside the jurisdiction of the Department of the Interior, at the urging of Muñoz; in 1961, President Kennedy issued an executive order ruling that all future "matters affecting Puerto Rico should be referred directly to the Office of the President." By encouraging this change, Muñoz placed more political weight than ever on the relationship between the chief executives in Washington and San Juan.

Federal Justice and Cerro Maravilla

The Cerro Maravilla killings of two young *independentistas* in 1978 and the ensuing investigations cast light on the workings of the federal judiciary system on the island. As with many other abuses of the system in Puerto Rico, the case was pursued only when it became a workable partisan issue. That occurred in the November 1982 elections, when the Popular Democratic Party took control of the Senate. Senate President Miguel Hernández Agosto launched an independent investigation, whose starting point was material uncovered by the *San Juan Star*. Public televised hearings began in 1983 and overthrew the findings of earlier investigations that had exonerated the police. The Senate hearings revealed a long-planned entrapment of the victims, approved by the highest levels of the Puerto Rican government, and cold-blooded murders that had been covered up for more than five years.

At the heart of the issue are the various official attitudes toward the violent wing of the Puerto Rican independence movement. For former Governor Carlos Romero Barceló, pro-Castro left-wing violence from the independence movement was one of his more effective arguments for the statehood movement. For the FBI, *independentista* violence is understood in the mainland context of organized crime and the international context of terrorism, but there is little analysis of the independence movement, its background, and its part in Puerto Rican intellectual and cultural life. The FBI has worked closely with the Puerto Rican police in anti-*independentista* efforts, including a number of "dirty tricks" carried out against the legal, electoral wing of the movement under the COINTELPRO plan of the 1960s and early 1970s. Vestiges of these attitudes are apparent in the FBI's conduct during two U.S. Department of Justice investigations into Cerro Maravilla between 1978 and 1980.

Authorities in Washington began to question the need for a federal investigation soon after the killings took place. The FBI was reluctant to investigate; on March 4, 1979, an FBI memo circulated in the Washington office said that the usual investigative procedure for such cases should be curtailed in this instance. Instead of "interviewing complainant, and the obtaining of police, coroner's or autopsy records, in addition to interviewing witnesses and subjects," the memo recommended that investigators limit their information to newspaper articles and the report of the Puerto Rican Department of Justice.

The U.S. Department of Justice is still not entirely out of the woods. In 1984, the department, under pressure from the Puerto Rican Senate findings, at last came through with grand jury indictments on the case. They dealt only with the cover-up—for the statute of limitations had run out on the killings—and they were limited to ten police agents, with no mention of higher Romero administration officials. The trial has been postponed repeatedly by the federal judge in San Juan; one frustrated Justice Department prosecutor described the delay as "extraordinarily strange."

Justice has been gravely delayed—if not miscarried—in the Cerro Maravilla case. Justice Department officials insist that the truth is more prosaic, although the implications may be ultimately more sinister. The Justice Department investigations, they say, were limited by the biased and second-rate investigatory efforts of the FBI.

And the federal authorities themselves are limited by Puerto Rico's rampant political polarization. Within the fifty states, the federal judiciary system can act as a check on abuses of power by state officials. In Puerto Rico, federal authorities are wary of getting involved in issues that may turn out to be power struggles between factions. The passion and the political machinations surrounding the status issue represent dangerous and uncharted waters; in dubious cases, it has been easier for Washington officials to look the other way than to test their jurisdiction.

Puerto Rican National Guardsmen in the Central American Conflict

The National Guard of Puerto Rico, like the units of the fifty states, are officially under the command of the governor and have a mandate to defend the U.S. national frontiers. At the same time, the Puerto Rican National Guard has occupied a special position, both in relation to U.S. military goals in the Caribbean region and in the island's relation to the federal government.

The Guard was created in 1919 and went into active duty in 1940 as the 295th Infantry Regiment, serving primarily in the Caribbean and Panama. The wartime mobilization of Puerto Rican servicemen coincided with a period of intense frustration over the failure to expand Puerto Rican powers of self-government. Washington did not leap to the conclusion that an island providing fighting men deserved greater representation; in fact, the U.S. Navy, protective of the political environment surrounding its bases in Puerto Rico, even opposed the idea of an elective governor.

Since the onset of the current crisis in Central America, the role of the Puerto Rican National Guard has been carefully reconsidered by the Pentagon. Puerto Rico has served a manifold purpose in the U.S. military expansion in the Caribbean of the early 1980s. First, the bases on the island itself have assumed more importance than ever, both as the strongholds of the "Caribbean Malta" and as the staging grounds for major exercises, such as "Ocean Venture," which took place in the summer of 1984. Second, Puerto Rican National Guardsmen are used as a liaison unit to strengthen the possibilities for joint field operations with other military forces in the region.

Conclusion

It is obvious that no one is satisfied with Puerto Rico's current status— except Washington. For the moment, commonwealth status allows Washington to control the questions that confront Puerto Rico in a one-sided manner. All of Puerto Rico's political parties have sought amendments of one kind or another their status, but until now the realm of possibility for their proposals has been hypothetical. The Puerto Ricans have no channels to press their desire for change until they achieve a public consensus, but under current conditions consensus may be unreachable. And there is no guarantee that if the Puerto Ricans did reach a momentary consensus on status, the decision would be honored.

For the time being, Puerto Rico remains at a classic stalemate. Most of the inequities of the current system favor Washington over the interests of Puerto Rico. But the inequities are not intolerable enough for the Puerto Ricans to challenge them in a definitive way.

19

Puerto Rican Politics and National Political Parties

Mark L. Schneider
Pan American Health Organization

A t the Democratic Presidential Convention in San Francisco in July 1984, the roll call reached the delegation of Puerto Rico and Governor Carlos Romero Barceló, leader of the island's New Progressive Party (PNP), responded, "Madame Secretary, the fifty-three delegates from the next state of the Union, the fifty-first state, Puerto Rico, cast their votes for their choice for the Democratic nomination." A month later, at the Republican Presidential Convention in Dallas, the same moment arrived and the chairman of the Puerto Rican delegation, former Governor Luis Ferré, also a leader of the PNP and also a statehood advocate, intoned: "The delegation of Puerto Rico casts all of its fourteen votes for its choice for the Republican candidate." How could the former and present governors of the Commonwealth of Puerto Rico, both from the same party and both statehood advocates, lead the delegations in the same year to *both* national party presidential conventions?

A glance at the makeup of the 1980 Puerto Rican delegation to the Democratic Presidential Convention merely adds to the confusion. A majority of twenty-one votes was cast for President Carter by PNP Governor Romero Barceló's designate, while a minority of twenty votes was cast for Senator Edward M. Kennedy by the representative of former Governor Rafael Hernández Colón, the 1980 Popular Democratic Party's nominee against Governor Romero Barceló.

Those somewhat bizarre episodes reflect the ambiguities, contradictions and complexities of the relationship between Puerto Rico's political parties and the national two-party system. Present Puerto Rican involvement in the national Democratic and Republican parties is largely hostage to the central issue of Puerto Rican politics—the character of that island's link to the United States. Ptolemaic and Copernican apostles may have been willing to die in the debate over whether the earth was the center of the universe. The debate in Puerto Rico is over whether one believes in a future independent nation, a fifty-first state, or "expanded" commonwealth. That question looms as the preeminent factor of Puerto Rican politics and, as such, the major influence on the way the political parties there relate to the national party structure. The national political parties have responded only vaguely to the increased polarization within Puerto Rico, a polarization clearly evident in the bare 3,000-plus vote margin of victory for Governor Romero Barceló out of 1.6 million votes cast in 1980.

The local party system in Puerto Rico is divided among the Popular Democratic Party (PPD), which supports commonwealth and was the dominant party for some three decades; the New Progressive Party (PNP), which advocates statehood; the newly formed Puerto Rican Renewal Party (PRP), a splinter of the NPP based on the gubernatorial candidacy of Dr. Hernán Padilla, former mayor of San Juan; and the two minor (at least in numbers) parties supporting independence, the Puerto Rican Independence Party (PIP) and the more radical Puerto Rican Socialist Party (PSP). The PSP officially lost its registration because of its failure to win an adequate share of the votes in 1980.

The history of local Puerto Rican parties has been tumultuous and explosive. Until 1940, the panoply of political parties vying for their share of local power was described by Robert W. Anderson as one in which "charisma supersedes ideology, personal authority overrides institutional responsibility, pragmatic commitment to change in and for itself far outweighs an ideological commitment. . . . And if ambiguity is a virtue, then Puerto Rico is a most virtuous society."[1]

The Union Party of Puerto Rico was formed in 1904 and incorporated both statehood and independence in its platform. By 1913, it reduced the acceptable alternatives to "complete independence, independence as an American protectorate, or a transitory status of autonomy."[2]

The postwar party structure in Puerto Rico was changed in every possible way by the victorious emergence of the Popular Democratic Party in 1940. As the distinguished Puerto Rican historian Arturo Morales Carrión has written: "Under the dynamic leadership of Luis Muñoz Marín, the PPD in 1944 moved decisively to the center of Puerto Rico's political stage, a position it would occupy for a quarter of a century."[3] The PPD became the vehicle through which Muñoz directed the transformation of Puerto Rico in an effort to end the economic dependence of the island and to combine that development with a new expression of national autonomy.[4]

The other constant in the Puerto Rican Republican party firmament has been statehood. It has remained the lodestar for the definition of the Republican party identity. Throughout the years of the New Deal, a time when the relatively close personal relationship between Muñoz and President Roosevelt and his advisors implied a special relationship, there was divided opinion on whether to create a Puerto Rican Democratic party affiliate to compete for a share of local power. The ties between Muñoz and the Populares and the national Democratic party leadership grew stronger across the years. It was with the support of the New Deal coalition remaining with President Harry Truman that the Elective Governor Act was approved in 1947 and Public Law 600 was adopted in 1950. Public Law 600 provided for a referendum on status (the commonwealth concept was approved by 76 percent of those voting) and permitted Puerto Rico to develop its own constitution and submit it to the Congress for approval. In this way, Puerto Rico freely associated with the United States in a new compact.

President Kennedy saw Puerto Rico as a test for U.S. policy toward Latin America and an opportunity to demonstrate that there were other paths beside violent revolution to modernize societies. He felt that Muñoz and the Populares were blazing a new and different trail in Puerto Rico. He was the first American president to travel to Puerto Rico, where a huge popular reception was organized by the Populares. Kennedy also appointed Populares leaders to high federal positions, particularly Teodoro Moscoso as the first head of the Alliance for Progress and Arturo Morales Carrión as a deputy assistant secretary of state for inter-American affairs. In these events, additional links were placed into the chain binding together the PPD and the national Democratic Party.[5]

Every four years, the Puerto Rican Republican party and the Democratic organization recognized by the national party as the legitimate party affiliate has sent delegates to the national presidential conventions. There has also been close involvement with national executive and congressional leaders as local parties maintained their own man in Washington to lobby for Puerto Rican concerns and interests. Bills calling for statehood and independence were continually introduced during the 1970s. The resident commissioner in the House of Representatives, with voice but no vote except in committee, also embodies a permanent link to the political powers that be in Washington.

In 1976, then-challenger Jimmy Carter joined a group of local statehood political advocates who were pursuing their own agenda of breaking the iron grip of the PPD on the linkage to the national Democratic party. The insurgents managed to win a significant share of delegates, despite the traditional Democratic organization and PPD leadership support for the candidacy of Senator Henry ("Scoop") Jackson, whose Senate Interior Committee chairmanship had brought him into close contact with the local PPD apparatus over many years.[6]

Once elected, President Carter dispensed patronage through the "new" Democratic party affiliate leadership, particularly Franklin Delano López, who was aligned with the PNP and committed to the goal of statehood. López, who initially had used the local ADA chapter as his base of operations, with the support of former Governor Romero Barceló, grafted a separate line of communication, influence, and political power into the Democratic party. The traditional PPD leadership of Rafael Hernández Colón maintained its strong ties to a wider spectrum of representatives and senators and sought to regain their dominant voice within Democratic party machinery, arguing that those "new Democratic" interlopers were illegitimate, unconverted Republicans in Democratic clothing. The Romero Barceló response was that they had always been Democrats but had participated in Republican party activities because the Democratic party was sewed up by the PPD activists and seemingly committed to commonwealth.

The internal dynamics of the PPD actually complicated the attempt to regain monopoly control of the link to the national Democrats. The traditional PPD emphasis on autonomy and on commonwealth as an embodiment of that autonomy led to a spirited debate on the implications of involving the PPD directly in national Democratic party affairs, which seemed to imply less rather than greater autonomy from the U.S. political system. That ideological posture, along with the recognition that it would be an uphill battle against the combined forces of an opposition governor and a hostile president, resulted in the PPD abstaining from direct participation in the 1978 special primary to vote on Democratic delegates to the Democratic National Committee.[7]

Both the 1980 and 1984 contests emphasize the different kinds of potential inherent in the Puerto Rican primary. It constitutes the means to obtain a large bloc of delegates at a relatively early period during the primary season. At the same time, each of the major parties examines its own participation in light of the impact on local political fortunes. In that context, the primary represents the preliminary bout for the two parties to get a feel for each other's strengths and weaknesses before the November gubernatorial main event.

For the Republican party, 1980 also saw a wide-open primary battle in which George Bush overwhelmed the forces of Senator Howard Baker and John Connolly. Ronald Reagan's Puerto Rican presence was almost nonexistent during that contest. However, the delegation sent to the Republican presidential convention has been one of the smallest, and the interest of the presidential candidates has therefore been minor. However, just as with the Democratic process, the choice of the delegation to the Republican convention is seen in terms of its impact on the local parties. Thus, in 1984, Mayor Hernán Padilla challenged Governor Ferré for the right to control the delegation to the convention. Only a court decision determined the outcome, in which the PNP's old guard lost its 16-year monopoly grip on the party machinery. Padilla's PRP took six of the fourteen delegates, and former Governor Ferré had to be content with the other eight delegates.

The key shift in the past 10 years has been the appearance of a strong statehood faction, composed of PNP advocates, within the Democratic party. Their success translated into patronage during the Carter years, dominance in the 1984 convention, and an end to the strong support for commonwealth in party statements on the status question.

Since 1952, the Democratic party platforms had praised commonwealth as the expressed desire of the people of Puerto Rico. They not only accepted commonwealth as a legitimate, noncolonial status but lauded it as a unique political invention, affording autonomy without breaking the ties with the United States. They had accepted the plebiscite results of 1967, when commonwealth status, with Muñoz leading the charge, received 60.5 percent of the vote. In 1972, the platform went further, including language supporting the Puerto Rican people's right *"to freely associate* in permanent union with the United States, as an *autonomous* commonwealth" (emphasis added) and accepting the PPD's new stance in favor of a continuing evolution of the relationship stressing "expanded commonwealth," affording greater autonomy to the island.

The arrival of the statehooders in 1976 marked a significant shift. Commonwealth was not singled out but was forced to share mention with statehood as legitimate and acceptable choices for a future expression of self-determination by the people of Puerto Rico. In 1972, statehood was not mentioned, and commonwealth—including the most recent refinements of PPD party positions—was endorsed emphatically. In 1976, statehood edged onto the stage. Once the commonwealth monopoly had been broken in 1976, the logic of emphasizing the philosophical equivalence of the three choices for the future status of Puerto Rico—commonwealth, statehood, or independence—dominated the platform decision making. The Republican party, while acknowledging the right of the people of Puerto Rico to self-determination, has always endorsed statehood as the only appropriate ultimate choice for the island.[8]

The second element marking a shift in the role of Puerto Rico in national party politics is visible for all to see. In 1972, there were seven members of the Puerto Rican delegation among the 3,016 total votes at the Democratic National Convention. By 1976, the delegation had more than tripled to twenty-two, while the convention declined slightly to 3,008 delegates. Overall numbers of convention delegates rose by 18 percent. Between 1972 and 1984, the total number of delegates had grown by 30 percent, while the size of the Puerto Rican delegation had expanded more than 650 percent.[9] That change has meant that Puerto Rico's delegation on the floor of the 1984 Democratic convention was larger than that of twenty-five states. On the standing committees as well, Puerto Rican representation was greater than or equal to that of thirty-three states. For presidential aspirants, the potential importance of the Puerto Rican primary is clear. It can offer a large bloc of delegates to a candidate who is able to harness the local party apparatus of the island effectively.

An additional element is the high visibility of the Hispanic vote. Given the high voter participation in Puerto Rico, where the average turnout has been approximately 80 percent of those eligible,[10] the possibility of greatly increasing the Puerto Rican vote in the various states should be obvious. The major parties are cognizant of that fact, and the heavy focus by the Democratic party on registering Hispanic voters reflects that knowledge. With some two-thirds of the Hispanic vote unregistered and only 30 percent of those registered going to the polls, the Democratic party in particular looks with enormous yearning at the impact around the country of a high Hispanic turnout.

There has been a major shift in the relationship between Puerto Rico and the mainland in economic terms over the past decade, with changes that have inevitable political consequences. When perhaps half of all Puerto Rican citizens are receiving food stamps valued at nearly $1 billion, when nearly another $1 billion is received in school lunch funding and $1 billion in social security transfer payments—not to mention Medicaid and Medicare—there is an enormous dependency in effect. Politically, in Puerto Rico and particularly in Washington, there is little recognition of Puerto Rican payments to the federal treasury, which offset nearly half of those transfer payments, although only a third of the total federal distribution to Puerto Rico.[11]

The modern relationship among the parties has been shifting, affected by changes in the power relationship of the local parties as statehooders infiltrated and took over a large share of the communication lines to the national Democratic party. Changes in the rules of the Democratic party, which suddenly vaulted Puerto Rico's delegation into the category of an important primary prize, also has altered the relationship of the parties. And although the impacts are not fully visible, both the rising star of the Hispanic vote in domestic U.S. politics and the increasing economic importance of individual transfer payments may shift the past tendency for the relationship to be determined almost solely by local party dynamics and the issue of political status.

When that situation is combined with the restrictions placed on Puerto Rico—requiring that goods be transported in far higher-cost American ships, limiting many of those transfer payments and other federal programs to Puerto Rico, preventing any tariff decisions by the local government, and providing greater benefits through the Caribbean Basic Initiative to other Caribbean islands but not to Puerto Rico—then the reverse side of that relationship is evident.

Notes

1. Robert W. Anderson, *Party Politics in Puerto Rico* (Stanford, Calif.: Stanford University Press, 1965), p. 16.
2. Ibid., p. 49.

3. Arturo Morales Carrion, *Puerto Rico: A Political and Cultural History* (New York: Norton, 1983), p. 256.

4. Bolivar Pagan, *Historia de los Partidos Políticos Puertorriqueños, 1895–1956,* Vol. I (San Juan, Puerto Rico: Libreria Campos, pp. 113–114 (unofficial translation).

5. Raymond Carr, *Puerto Rico: A Colonial Experiment* (New York and London: New York University Press, 1984), pp. 72–104; and Carrion, *Puerto Rico,* pp. 256–309.

6. Carr, *Puerto Rico,* p. 67.

7. Unpublished transcript of the Committee on State Participation of the Democratic National Committee, August 31, 1982, pp. 21–33.

8. *National Party Platforms, 1960–1976,* Vol. II compiled by Donald Bruce Johnson (Urbana: University of Illinois Press); and 1980 and 1984 Republican and Democratic party platforms.

9. *Official Proceedings of the Democratic National Convention, 1972, 1976, 1980* (Washington, D.C.: Democratic National Committee) and *Final Call: The Democratic National Convention, 1984,* July 15, 1983, issued by the Democratic National Committee.

10. Bayron Toro, *Elecciones y Partidos Políticos de Puerto Rico, 1809–1976* (Mayaguez, Puerto Rico: Editorial Isla, 1977), p. 278.

11. United States Department of Commerce, *Economic Study of Puerto Rico: Vol. 1. Report to the President,* prepared by the Interagency Task Force, December 1979, pp. 159–174.

Appendix A
Excerpts from U.S. Treaties and Legislation Relating to Puerto Rico

Excerpts from the Treaty of Paris between the United States and Spain, as It Relates to Puerto Rico[a]

Concluded at Paris December 10, 1898; ratification advised by the Senate February 6, 1899; ratified by the President February 6, 1899; ratifications exchanged April 11, 1899; proclaimed April 11, 1899.

Article II. Spain ceded to the United States the island of Porto Rico and other islands now under Spanish sovereignty in the West Indies. . . .

Article III. . . . The United States will pay to Spain the sum of twenty million dollars ($20,000,000) within three months after the exchange of the ratifications of the present treaty. . . .

Article VIII. . . . In conformity with the provision of Articles I, II and III of this treaty, Spain relinquishes in Cuba and cedes in Porto Rico and the other islands of the West Indies . . . all the buildings, wharves, barrackes, forts, structure, public highways and other immobile property which, in conformity with the law, belong to the public domain. . . .

Excerpts from the Foraker Act of 1900, April 12, 1900, 56th Congress, 1st Session[b]

That the provisions of this Act shall apply to the island of Porto Rico. . . .

Sec. 6. That the capital Porto Rico shall be at the city of San Juan and the seat of government shall be maintained there. . . .

---

[a]*Source:* Clive Parry, ed., *The Consolidated Treaty Series (1898–1899)*, Vol. 187 (Dobbs Ferry, N.Y.: Oceana, 1979), pp. 100–105.

[b]*Source:* U.S. *Statutes at Large*, Vol. 31 (Washington, D.C.: Government Printing Office, 1901), pp. 77–86.

Sec. 7. That all inhabitants continuing to reside therein who were Spanish subjects on the eleventh day of April, eighteen hundred and ninety-nine and then resided in Porto Rico . . . shall be deemed and held to be citizens of Porto Rico and as such entitled to the protection of the United States. . . .

Sec. 11. That for the purpose of retiring the Porto Rican coins now in circulation . . . the Secretary of the Treasury [of the United States] is hereby authorized to redeem . . . at the present established rate of sixty cents in the coins of the United States for one peso of Porto Rican coin. . . .

Sec. 15. That the legislative authority hereinafter provided shall have power by due enactment to amend, alter, modify, or repeal any law or ordinance, civil or criminal, continued in force by this Act, as it may from time to time see fit.

Sec. 16. That all judicial process shall run in the name of "United States of America, ss: the President of the United States," and all criminal or penal prosecutions . . . shall be conducted in the name and by the authority of "The people of Porto Rico;" and all officials authorized by this Act shall before entering upon the duties of their respective offices take an oath to support the Constitution of the United States and the laws of Porto Rico.

The Governor

Sec. 17. That the official title of the chief executive officer shall be "The Governor of Porto Rico." He shall be appointed by the President, by and with the advise and consent of the Senate; he shall hold his office for a term of four years and until his successor is chosen and qualified unless sooner removed by the President. . . .

The Executive Council

Sec. 18. That there shall be appointed by the President, by and with the advice and consent of the Senate, for the period of four years, unless sooner removed by the President, a secretary, an attorny-general, a treasurer, an auditor, a commissioner of the interior, and a commissioner of education, each of who shall reside in Porto Rico during his official incombency . . . and who, together with five other persons . . . appointed by the President for a like term of four years, by and with the advice and consent of the Senate, shall constitute an executive council, at least five of whom shall be native inhabitants of Porto Rico. . . .

House of Delegates

Sec. 27. That all local legislative powers hereby granted shall be vested in a legislative assembly which shall consist of two houses; one the executive council . . . and the other a house of delegates, to consist of thirty-five members elected biennially by the qualified voters . . . and the two houses thus consisted shall be designated "The legislative assembly of Porto Rico."

The Judiciary

Sec. 33. That the judicial power shall be vested in the courts and tribunals of Porto Rico as already established and now in operation, including municipal courts . . . including also police courts. . . .

Sec. 39. That the qualified voters of Porto Rico shall . . . choose a resident commissioner to the United States. . . .

Excerpts from the Jones Act, March 2, 1917, H.R. 9533, 64th Congress, 2nd Session[c]

Be it enacted by the Senate and House of Representatives of the United States of America in Congress assembled, That the provisions of this Act shall apply to the island of Porto Rico. . . .

Bill of Rights

Sec. 2. That no law shall be enacted in Porto Rico which shall deprive any person of life, liberty or property without due process of law, or deny to any person therein the equal protection of the laws. . . .

Nothing contained in this Act shall be construed to limit the power of the legislature to enact laws for protection of the lives, health or safety of employees.

That no law shall be passed abridging the freedom of speech or of the press, or right of the people peaceably to assemble and petition the Government for redress of grievances.

That no law shall be made respecting an establishment of religion or prohibiting the free exercise thereof, and that the free exercise and enjoyment of religious profession and worship without discrimination or preference shall forever be allowed, and that no political or religious test other than

---

[c]*Source: U.S. Statutes at Large,* Vol. 34 (Washington, D.C.: Government Printing Office, 1918), pp. 951–68.

oath to support the Constitution of the United States and the laws of Porto Rico shall be required as a qualification to any office or public trust under the government of Porto Rico.

Sec. 3. That no export duties shall be levied or collected on exports from Porto Rico, but taxes and assessments on property, internal revenue and license fees and royalties for franchises privelages, and concessions may be imposed for the purposes of the insular and municipal governments . . . may be provided and defined by the Legislature of Porto Rico. . . .

Sec. 4. That the capital of Porto Rico shall be at the city of San Juan, and the seat of government shall be maintained there.

Sec. 5. That all citizens of Porto Rico are hereby declared, and shall be deemed and held to be citizens of the United States; *Provided* That any person . . . may retain his present political status by making a declaration, under oath, of his decision to do so within six months of the taking effect of this Act before the district court in the district in which he resides. . . .

Sec. 57. That the laws and ordinances of Porto Rico now in force shall continue in force and effect, except as altered, amended or repealed by the legislative authority herein provided for Porto Rico or by Act of Congress of United States. . . .

Excerpts from Public Law 600, Senate Resolution 3336, July 3, 1950[d]

. . . *Be it enacted by the Senate and House of Representatives of the United States of America in Congress assembled,* That . . . this Act is now adopted in the nature of a compact so that the people of Puerto Rico may organize a government pursuant to a constitution of their own adoption.

Sec. 2. This Act shall be submitted to the qualified voters of Puerto Rico for acceptance or rejection through an island-wide referendum to be held in accordance with the laws of Puerto Rico. Upon the approval of this Act, by a majority of the voters participating . . . the Legislature of Puerto Rico is authorized to call a constitutional convention to draft a constitution for the said island of Puerto Rico. The said constitution shall provide a republican form of government and shall include a bill of rights. . . . Upon approval

[d]*Source: U.S. Statutes at Large,* Vol. 64 (Washington, D.C.: Government Printing Office, 1951), pp. 319–20.

by the Congress the constitution shall become effective in accordance with its terms. . . .

Excerpts from Public Law 447, Joint Resolution 430ᵉ

. . . *Resolved by the Senate and the House of Representatives of the United States of America in Congress assembled,* That the constitution of the Commonwealth of Puerto Rico which was drafted by the selected delegates to the Constitutional Convention of Puerto Rico and adopted by the people of Puerto Rico in a referendum of March 3, 1952. . . .

. . . The constitution of the Commonwealth of Puerto Rico hereby approved shall be effective when the Constitutional Convention of Puerto Rico shall have declared in a formal resolution its acceptance in the name of the people of Puerto Rico of the conditions of approval herein contained, and when the Governor of Puerto Rico, being duly notified that such resolution of acceptance has been formally adopted, shall issue a proclamation to that effect. . . .

ᵉ*Source: U.S. Statutes at Large,* Vol. 66 (Washington, D.C.: Government Printing Office, 1953), pp. 327–28.

Appendix B

Puerto Rico's Election Results, 1960–84 (% of Total)

Party	1960	1964	1968	1972	1976	1980	1984
Statehood Republican Party[a]	32.1	34.7	0.5	—	—	—	—
New Progressive Party	—	—	43.06	43.4	48.8	47.23	44.62
Puerto Rican Renewal Party	—	—	—	—	—	—	4.06
Popular Democratic Party	58.2	59.2	40.7	50.7	45.3	47.03	47.76
Peoples Party[a]	—	—	11.7	0.3	—	—	—
Independence Party	3.1	2.8	3.5	5.4	6.4	—	3.56
Christian Action Party[a]	6.6	3.3	—	—	—	—	—
Others	—	—	—	0.2	—	—	—

Source: 1970 Census Figures: Office of Federal Affairs, Washington, D.C., and Commonwealth of Puerto Rico, 1985.

Note: The percentages are of a total of 1,722,706 votes.

[a]Party is now dissolved.

Select Bibliography

Gabrielle S. Brussel

Books

Anderson, Robert W. *Party Politics in Puerto Rico.* Stanford, Calif.: Stanford University Press, 1965.

Bloomfield, Richard, ed. *Puerto Rico: The Search for National Policy.* Westview Series on Latin America and Caribbean. Boulder, Colo.: Westview Press, 1985.

Cabranes, José A. *Citizenship and the American Empire: Notes on the Legislative History of the U.S. Citizenship of Puerto Ricans.* New Haven: Yale University Press, 1979.

Carr, Raymond. *Puerto Rico: A Colonial Experiment.* A Twentieth Century Fund Study. New York: Vintage Books/Random House, 1984.

Cordasco, Francesco; Bucchioni, Eugene; and Castellanos, Diego. *Puerto Ricans on the Mainland: A Bibliography of Reports, Texts, Critical Studies and Related Materials.* Totowa, N.J.: Rowman and Littlefield, 1972.

Cripps, Louis L. *Puerto Rico: The Case for Independence.* Cambridge, Mass.: Schenkman, 1974.

De Beers, John S. *A Study of Puerto Rico's Banking System.* San Juan, Puerto Rico: Financial Council of Puerto Rico, 1960.

Dominguez, Virginia R., and Dominguez, Jorge I. *The Caribbean: Its Implications for the United States.* Headline Series 253. New York: Foreign Policy Association, February 1981.

Epica Task Force. *Puerto Rico: A People Challenging Colonialism: A People's Primer by EPICA Task Force.* Washington, D.C.: EPICA Task Force, 1970.

Estefano Pisani, Miguel A. *Puerto Rico: Análisis de un plebiscito.* Havana: Tricontinental, 1968.

Falk, Pamela S. *Puerto Rico: Political Labyrinth.* Boulder, Colo.: Westview Press, 1986.

Farr, Kenneth. *Personalism and Party Politics: Institutionalization of the Popular Democratic Party of Puerto Rico.* Hato Rey, Puerto Rico: Inter American University Press, 1975.

Freyre, Jorge F. *External and Domestic Financing in the Economic Development of Puerto Rico.* Rio Piedras, Puerto Rico: Editorial Universitaria, 1969.

García Passalacqua, Juan Manuel. *Puerto Rico: Equality and Freedom at Issue in the Caribbean.* New York: Praeger, 1984.

Golding, Morton J. *A Short History of Puerto Rico*. New York: New American Library, 1973.

Gordon, Raoul. *The Nationalist Movement in Puerto Rico*. New York: Gordon Press, 1976.

———. *Political Parties in Puerto Rico, 1898–1976*. New York: Gordon Press, 1976.

———, ed. *The Puerto Rican Culture*. New York: Gordon Press, 1976.

Hayden, Sherman S., and Rivlin, Benjamin. *Non-Self-Governing Territories: Status of Puerto Rico*. New York: Woodrow Wilson Foundation, 1954.

Heine, Jorge. *Time for Decision: The U.S. and Puerto Rico*. Lanham, Md.: North-South Publishers, 1984.

Heine, Jorge, and García Passalacqua, Juan M. *The Puerto Rican Question*. Headline Series 266. New York: Foreign Policy Association, November/December 1983.

History Task Force. *Labor Migration under Capitalism: The Puerto Rican Experience*. Project by the Centro de Estudios Puertorriquenos, City University of New York. New York: Monthly Review Press, 1979.

Holbrook, Robert S. *A Study of the Characteristics, Behavior and Implications of "Possessions Corporations" in Puerto Rico*. Washington, D.C.: U.S. Department of the Treasury, 1977.

Ickes, Harold L. *The Secret Diaries of Harold L. Ickes* (3 vols.). New York: Simon and Schuster, 1954.

Johnson, Roberta Ann. *Puerto Rico: Commonwealth or Colony?* New York: Praeger, 1980.

Lacovara, Philip A. *The Authority of the Commonwealth of Puerto Rico under the U.S. Constitution to Join International Organizations and to Enter into International Agreements*. Hato Rey, Puerto Rico: Inter American University Press, 1971.

Leibowitz, Arnold H. *Colonial Emancipation in the Pacific and the Caribbean: A Legal and Political Analysis*. New York: Praeger, 1976.

Lewis, Gordon K. *Puerto Rico: A Case Study in the Problems of Contemporary American Federalism*. Port-of-Spain, Trinidad: Office of the Premier of Trinidad and Tobago, 1960.

———. *Puerto Rico: Freedom and Power in the Caribbean*. New York: Harper and Row, 1968.

Morales Carrión, Arturo. *Puerto Rico: A Political and Cultural History*. New York: Norton, 1983.

Muñoz Marín, Luis. *Collected Speeches of Luis Muñoz Marín, July 25, 1952–August 28, 1957*. An unpublished collection. Gainsville: University of Florida at Gainsville.

National Academy of Public Administration. *Strengthening the Executive Branch of the Commonwealth of Puerto Rico*. San Juan: National Academy of Public Administration, 1971.

Perl, Lila. *Puerto Rico: Island Between Two Worlds*. New York: Morrow, 1979.

Perloff, Harvey S. *Puerto Rico's Economic Future: A Study in Planned Development*. New York: Ayer, 1975.

Reisman, Michael. *Puerto Rico and the International Process: New Roles in Asso-

ciation. Studies in Transnational Legal Policy No. 6. Washington, D.C.: American Society of International Law, 1975.

Romero Barceló, Carlos. *Statehood Is for the Poor*. San Juan: Private printing, 1978.

Roosevelt, Theodore. *Colonial Policies of the U.S.* (Introduction by Walter Lippmann). Garden City, N.Y.: Doubleday, 1937.

Sevrana Geyls, Raul. *The Territorial Status of Puerto Rico and Its Effect on the Political Future of the Island*. New York: Columbia University Press, 1945.

Stead, William H. *FOMENTO—The Economic Development of Puerto Rico*. Washington, D.C.: National Planning Association, 1958.

Supreme Court of Puerto Rico. *Rules of Evidence, 1979*. San Juan: Supreme Court of Puerto Rico, 1981.

Tugswell, Rexford G. *Puerto Rico Public Papers of R. G. Tugswell, Governor*. New York: Arno Press, 1975.

———. *Stricken Land, The Story of Puerto Rico* (Reproduction of 1946 edition). New York: Greenwood, 1968.

Trias Mongé, José. *Historia Constitucional de Puerto Rico* (Vol. 1). Rio Piedras: University of Puerto Rico Press, 1980.

———. *Historia Constitucional de Puerto Rico* (Vols. 2 and 3). Rio Piedras: University of Puerto Rico Press, 1981.

Wells, Henry. *Government Financing of Political Parties in Puerto Rico*. Princeton: Citizens' Research Foundation, 1961.

———. *The Modernization of Puerto Rico: A Political Study of Changing Values and Institution*. Cambridge, Mass.: Harvard University Press, 1969.

Zavala, Iris M., and Rodríguez, Rafael, eds. *The Intellectual Roots of Independence: An Anthology of Puerto Rican Political Essays*. New York: Monthly Review Press, 1980.

Articles

Berríos Martínez, Rubén. "Independence for Puerto Rico: The Only Solution." *Foreign Affairs* 55(April 1977): 561–83.

Bonilla, Frank, and Campos, Ricardo. "A Wealth of Poor: Puerto Ricans in the New Economic Order." *Daedalus* 110(1981): 133–76.

Cabranes, José A. "Puerto Rico: Out of the Colonial Closet." *Foreign Policy* 33(Winter 1978): 66–91.

Corrada del Río, Baltasar. "The Reagan Administration's (Economic) Policies and Puerto Rico." *Puerto Rico Business Review* 7(January/February 1982): 3–9.

Clerc, Jean Pierre. "Puerto Rico's Identity Crisis: Growing Dissension over a National Destiny (Statehood, Association or Independence)." *World Press Review* 27(June 1980): 32–34.

García Passalacqua, Juan Manuel. "The Alternative: A Federal Solution to the Colonial Problem." *Documentos Basicos*. Primer Instituto de Verano de Relaciones Internacionales, University of Puerto Rico, 1959, pp. 69–79.

———. "The Legality of the Associated Statehood of Puerto Rico." *Inter-American Law Review* 4(July–December 1962): 287–315.

————. "Los Nuevos Democratas: Un Analises Historico." *El Nuevo Dia,* Sunday Supplement, 3 December 1977, p. 5.

————. "La Reforma del Proceso Electoral de Puerto Rico." *Revista del Colegio de Abogados de Puerto Rico* 42(November 1981): 575–583.

Hernández Colón, Rafael. "The Commonwealth of Puerto Rico—Territory or State?" *Revista del Colegio de Abogados de Puerto Rico* 19(May 1959): 207–58.

Internal Revenue Service. Kenneth Szelflinski "U.S. Possessions Corporation Tax Credit, 1980." *Statistics of Income Bulletin Quarterly* (June 1983): 41–45.

Kiefer, Donald W. "Treating Puerto Rico as a State under Federal Tax and Expenditure Programs: A Preliminary Economic Analysis." Congressional Research Service, September 1977. Subsequently published in the *Revista del Colegio de Abogados de Puerto Rico* 39(November 1978): 657–85.

Madera, José. "Bigger Roles for Puerto Rico in Plans for Caribbean? Interview with Jose R. Madera, Administrator, Economic Development Administration, Puerto Rico," *U.S. News and World Report,* no. 92, 12 March 1982, pp. 93–94.

McDougall, George. "The Case for the 51st State." *Newsweek,* 10 March 1980, p. 21.

Morales Carrion, A. "Puerto Rico and the U.S.: A Historian's Perspective." *Revista del Colegio de Abogades de Puerto Rico* 42(November 1981): 585–663.

Muñoz Marín, Luis. "Plight of Puerto Rico." *Political Science Quarterly* 57(December 1942): 481–503.

————. "Puerto Rico and the United States: Their Future Together," *Foreign Affairs* 32(1954): 341–51.

————. "Breakthrough from Nationalism: A Small Island Looks at Big Trouble." The Godkin Lectures, Harvard University. San Juan, Puerto Rico: Office of the Governor, 1959.

————. "Puerto Rico Does Not Want to Be a State." *New York Times Magazine,* 16 Aug. 1945, pp. 35–40.

Nader, Ralph. "The Commonwealth Status in Puerto Rico." *Harvard Law Review* 33(13 Dec. 1956): 1–8.

Reagan, Ronald. "Puerto Rico and Statehood." *Wall Street Journal,* 11 Feb. 1980, p. 20.

"Recent Changes in the Possessions Corporation System of Taxation: Their Efficacy and Their Relationship to Puerto Rico's Economic Development." *Cornell International Law Journal* 16(Summer 1983): 431–68.

Romero Barceló, Carlos. "Puerto Rico, U.S.A.: The Case for Statehood." *Foreign Affairs* 59(Fall 1980): 60–81.

————. "Puerto Rico's Role in the Caribbean Basin." *Puerto Rico Business Review* 7(November 1982): 3–6.

Public Documents

U.S. Congress. House Banking, Finance and Urban Affairs Committee, *Puerto Rico and the Section 936 Tax Incentives: Hearings before the Subcommittee on Gen-*

eral Oversight and Renegotiation. 97th Cong., 2nd Sess. Washington, D.C.: GPO, 1982.

———. Subcommittee on General Oversight and Renegotiation, *Puerto Rico and the Section 936 Tax Incentives, December 15, 1982.* 97th Cong., 2nd Sess. Washington, D.C.: GPO, 1982.

U.S. Congress. House Committee on Interior and Insular Affairs. *Hearing before the Committee on Interior and Insular Affairs, 82nd Cong., 2nd Sess., on House Joint Resolution No. 430. A joint resolution approving the Constitution of the Commonwealth of Puerto Rico, which was adopted by the people of Puerto Rico.* Washington, D.C.: GPO, 1952.

———. *Relating to Self Determination for the People of Puerto Rico.* 96th Cong., 1st Sess. Washington, D.C.: GPO, 1979.

———. Subcommittee on Territorial and Insular Affairs. *Hearings on H.R. 9234, A Bill to Provide for Amendments to the Compact between the People of Puerto Rico and the United States, and Related Legislation.* 86th Cong., 1st Sess., December 1959. Washington, D.C.: GPO, 1959.

———. *Hearings on H.R. 5945, H.R. 5947, H.R. 5948, H.R. 5991, H.R. 6047, H.R. 6076, H.R. 6083, Bills to Establish a Procedure for the Prompt Settlement, in a Democratic Manner, of the Political Status of Puerto Rico.* 88th Cong., 1st Sess., May 1963. Washington, D.C.: GPO, 1963.

———. *Hearings on H.R. 11200 and H.R. 11201 to Approve the Compact of Permanent Union Between Puerto Rico and the United States.* 94th Congress, 2nd Sess., January 20 and February 9, 1976. Washington, D.C.: GPO, 1976.

U.S. Department of Commerce. *Economic Study of Puerto Rico: Report to the President Prepared by the Interagency Task Force Coordinated by the United States Department of Commerce,* Vol. I & II. Washington, D.C.: GPO, 1979.

Index

118 • *The Political Status of Puerto Rico*

Public works program, 20
Puerto Rican Economic Development
  Association, xi
Puerto Rican Independence party, xii–
  xiii, xiv, 11, 37, 94; on federal aid,
  47; international support, 37
Puerto Rican Renewal party, 94
Ruetro Rican Socialist party, 94
Puerto Rico Industrial Development
  Company (PRIDCO), 41
Puerto Rico Reconstruction Agency
  (PRRA) 41, 49
Puryear, Jeffrey, xiv, 3–14, 60

Racism, 35–36
Reagan, Ronald: economic policies, 44,
  45–46; and corporate taxes, 8; and
  enterprise zones, 72; and statehood
  for Puerto Rico, 59–60
Recession, 3
Republican party, xi, 93, 94
Revenue sharing funds, 29
Revenues, 26–27, 28–29
Rice project, 21
Romero Barceló, Carlos, xi, xiv, 31–
  34, 56, 60, 90, 93, 94
Roosevelt, Franklin D., 88, 94
Rulfo, Juan, 22
Rum, excise taxes, 17, 28, 50; and
  Caribbean Basin Initiative, 65–66

Saint Louis Post Dispatch, 60
San Juan, Pedro, 14 n. 8
San Juan Star, xiv, 96
Sánchez, Luis Rafael, xiii
School lunch program, 98
Section 936. *See* Internal Revenue
  Code, Section 936
Service industry, 42
Shame of the Cities, The (Steffens), 58
Simpson-Mazzoli immigration bill, 14
  n. 13
Small business financing, 22
Social security, 25, 45, 98
Socialist International, 10
Solar energy, 21
Spain, 4–5, 10, 25, 43, 85
Spanish language. *See* Language issue
Standard of living, 44, 46
Statehood: advantages, xi–xii, 16–18,
  31–34; economic effects, 25–29;

and language issue, 8–9, 17, 31–
  32; and media, 52–58; and national politics, 83–84, 94–98; obstacles to, xii, 36–37; and political
  parties, xi–xiii, xiv, 11, 12, 13, 91–
  92; Reagan on, 59–60; and state
  government, 28–29; and taxes, xii,
  17, 26; and U.S. Congress, xii, 6–7,
  9–10, 11–13, 32–33, 37, 86; *see
  also* Status issue
Status issue, 3, 6–7; and national parties, 83, 93–98; and political parties, xi–xii, xiv, 11, 12, 13, 91–92,
  93–99; referendum, xi, 3, 7, 12, 86,
  95; and United Nations, xiii, 3, 10,
  62–63; *see also* Commonwealth;
  Independence; Statehood
Steffens, Lincoln, 58
Subsidies, xi, xii–xiii; and business,
  42; *see also* Transfer payments
Sugar, 50
Supply-side economics, 49

Tax Equity and Fiscal Responsibility
  Act, 33
Tax policies, 25; corporation exemp-
  tions, xi, 8, 11, 17, 27, 41–42, 51–
  52, 66; and statehood, xii, 26, 27–
  28
Tax Reform Report, 73–74
Telephone service, excise tax, 26
Teller Amendment, 85
Textile industry, 66
Time, 57
Tourism, 49, 51
Transfer payments, xi, 3, 8, 45–46,
  52, 73, 75 n. 10; and gross domes-
  tic product, 45, 87; and statehood,
  29
Transportation costs, 45
Treaty of Paris, xiv, 4, 101
Treaty relations, 9
Truman, Harry S., 95
Tugwell, Rexford Guy, 41, 50, 51, 88
Twinning, 65, 66, 72, 75 n. 7
295th Infantry Regiment, 91

Unemployment, 3, 19, 20, 37, 44, 46;
  and Section 936 reform, 71, 78–79;
  and statehood, 26
Union Party of Puerto Rico, 94

About the Contributors

Hubert C. Barton (now deceased) was director of economic research and planning, Puerto Rico Planning Board, Economic Development Administration, and a member of the Puerto Rican legislature. He was also president of the Puerto Rico Development Group.

Rubén Berríos Martínez is a Senator in the legislature of Puerto Rico and a professor of law at the University of Puerto Rico. Mr. Berríos Martínez was also a member of the Senate of Puerto Rico from 1973 to 1977. He has been the head of the Puerto Rican Independence Party for 15 years and is the party's chief spokesman.

Gabrielle S. Brussel is a graduate student in international affairs at Columbia University. She has been the Americas Society's production manager for *Puerto Rico's Political Status* and worked as research associate for the Puerto Rico Project at the Americas Society.

Francisco A. Catalá is an associate professor at the University of Puerto Rico at Arecibo. He is a member of the Puerto Rican Independence Party.

Antonio J. Colorado Laguna is the administrator of the Economic Development Administration of Puerto Rico (FOMENTO). A specialist in corporations and taxation, he worked at FOMENTO from 1966 until 1973, first as the legal tax advisor on taxation to the administrator and then as the executive assistant to the administrator. He then went into private practice and from 1979 until 1984 was a member of Colorado, Martinez Odell, Calabria and Sierra. In 1985 he became administrator of the Economic Development Administration.

Baltasar Corrada del Río has been mayor of San Juan, Puerto Rico, since 1984. He was previously elected by the populace of Puerto Rico to serve as resident commissioner of Puerto Rico in the U.S. Congress. In this capacity, he served as a member of the Education and Labor Committee and the Interior and Insular Affairs Committee from 1977 until 1984.

Maurice A. Ferre, former mayor of Miami, served six successive terms—from 1973 until 1984—the only political candidate in Miami's history to do so. Mr. Ferre has also served in the Florida State Legislature, as a member of the Miami City Commission, on the President's Advisory Committee on Refugees, the Presidential Advisory Board on Ambassadorial Appointments, and in UNESCO General Assembly (Paris) between 1975 and 1978.

Robert Garcia is the representative to Congress for the Eighteenth Congressional District in New York. He has served in Congress since 1978 and is the chairman of the Subcommittee on Census and Population of the House Committee on Post Office and Civil Service. He is also a member of the House Committee on Banking, Finance and Urban Affairs and the House Foreign Relations Committee. Mr. Garcia is chairman of the Congressional Hispanic Caucus and sits on the House Democratic Steering and Policy Committee.

Juan Manuel García Passalacqua is a commentator and columnist for the *San Juan Star* and is legal counsel to the Ana G. Mendez Educational Foundation of Puerto Rico. He is the author of numerous articles and books on Puerto Rico's status; he is the coauthor of "The Puerto Rican Question," published by the Foreign Policy Association in 1983. Mr. García Passalacqua is a lawyer and was assistant to Puerto Rico's former Governors Luis Muñoz Marin and Roberto Sanchez Vilella as well as a member of the U.S. National Hispanic Advisory Group.

Edith Grossman, a critic and translator of Latin American literature, is the author of *The Antipoetry of Nicanor Parra.* Her work has appeared in various journals and publications and she has translated many major Latin American writers, including Nicanor Parra, Mario Vargas Llosa, Julio Cortazar, Guillermo Cabrera Infante, and Jacobo Timerman. Ms. Grossman teaches Spanish, humanities, and Latin American literature at Dominican College in Orangeburg, New York.

Miguel A. Hernández Agosto has been president of the Senate of Puerto Rico since 1981. In 1960, he was appointed executive director of the Puerto Rico Land Authority by Governor Luis Muñoz Marin. He has also served extensively in the Department of Agriculture and Commerce of Puerto Rico, first as assistant secretary of agriculture and from 1965 until 1968 as secretary of agriculture. His positions in the Senate have included senator-at-large, vice-president, and minority leader. Mr. Hernandez Agosto served as president of the Popular Democratic Party from 1973 until 1978.

Rafael Hernández Colón was elected governor of Puerto Rico in 1984. He also served in that capacity from 1972 until 1976. He has been the leader of the Popular Democratic Party (PDP) since 1969 and served as senator-at-Large, PDP, from 1969 until 1984. He also served as attorney general of the Puerto Rican Department of Justice from 1965 until 1967.

George W. Landau, president of the Americas Society, previously served as U.S. Ambassador to Venezuela (1982–85), Chile (1977–82), and Paraguay (1972–77). He received the Wilbur Carr Award for distinguished service as a career diplomat upon his retirement from the Department of State in 1985 and the Presidential Meritorious Award in 1984. Ambassador Landau is a member of the Council on Foreign Relations.

Stephen Lande, vice-president of Manchester Associates, is an international trade expert and a professional negotiator. From 1973 to 1982, he served as Assistant United States Trade Representative and Chief Negotiator for the United States Trade Representative (USTR). Mr. Lande established the bilateral relations section of USTR for developing overall U.S. strategy and for conducting negotiations between the United States and the developing countries, Eastern Europe, Canada, the European Communities, and Japan. He oversaw the conclusion of twenty-eight agreements with developing countries in the Multilateral Trade Negotiations and was responsible for implementation and administration of the Generalized System of Preference.

Theodore Lane is currently on leave from the University of Alaska while he serves as consultant to the Puerto Rican Economic Development Administration. In this capacity, he has been working to improve Puerto Rico's human resources programs and studying the impact of investment incentives on the demand for labor. Dr. Lane has also been working on Puerto Rico's proposal to use Section 936 funds to support twin-planting between Puerto Rico and the nations of the Caribbean. Previously, Dr. Lane was a partner in Lane/Langley and Associates, economic consultants.

José R. Madera Prado is former administrator of the Economic Development Administration, Government of Puerto Rico (FOMENTO). Mr. Madera served as the president of Governor's Interagency Committee on International Trade, and in 1976 became treasurer of Citibank's Puerto Rico Branch Office, in charge of operations in the U.S. Virgin Islands and Puerto Rico.

Russell E. Marks, Jr., senior vice-president of Haley Associates, was a president and founding officer of the Americas Society. Before joining the society, Mr. Marks was president of Phelps Dodge International, a wholly owned subsidiary of Phelps Dodge Corporation, New York, which had a subsidiary operation in Puerto Rico that qualified under the provisions of Section 936. There he supervised manufacturing operations in fifteen countries, including Mexico, Guatemala, Honduras, El Salvador, Costa Rica, Panama, Venezuela, Ecuador, and Chile.

George McDougall served as special assistant to the governor of Puerto Rico from 1976 until 1984. He has also served as a member of the San Juan Municipal Assembly and is a delegate to the General Assembly of Puerto Rico's New Progressive Party and a member of the New Progressive Party's San Juan Central Committee.

Teodoro Moscoso served Puerto Rico as the architect and organizer of the Economic Development Administration (FOMENTO), and as the president of the Puerto Rico Industrial Development Company from 1942 until 1961, when he was appointed U.S. Ambassador to Venezuela by President John Kennedy. From 1961 until 1964 he served as U.S. Coordinator of the Alliance for Progress. Dr. Moscoso is currently the chairman of Farmacias Moscoso and Banco de Santander-Puerto Rico.

Anne Nelson, a 1976 graduate of Yale University, has been writing about the Caribbean and Central America since 1978. Her articles have appeared in *Harper's* magazine, the *Los Angeles Times,* the *Columbia Journalism Review,* and a number of other publications. Her book on the Cerro Maravilla case in Puerto Rico, *Murder Under Two Flags,* will be published by Ticknor and Fields in 1986.

Hernán Padilla was elected mayor of San Juan for the first time in 1976 and served until 1984. He previously served eight years in the Puerto Rican House of Representatives as majority leader (1968–72) and as minority leader (1972–76). Mr. Padilla was a founding member of the New Progressive Party and began the Puerto Rican Renewal Party as an alternative to the three dominant parties competing in the 1984 election.

Jeffrey Puryear is currently the Southern Cone and Andean Zone representative of the Ford Foundation. He served previously as the foundation's program officer for the Caribbean and, during the 1970s, as program advisor in Peru, Argentina, and Chile. In 1978–79, Dr. Puryear was Visiting Fellow at Stanford University.

Carlos Romero Barceló was governor of Puerto Rico in 1976 and again in 1980. Previously, in 1968 and in 1972, he was mayor of San Juan. In 1974, Mr. Romero Barceló also became president of the New Progressive Party and in 1975 became the first Hispanic elected president of the U.S. National League of Cities. Mr. Romero Barceló was a co-founder of the pro-statehood New Progressive Party.

Luis Rafael Sánchez is a Puerto Rican novelist known for his innovative writing—specifically his "neon prose" on Puerto Rico's political culture. His recent works include a novel, *Macho Camacho's Beat;* an essay, "The Air Bus," in *Short Sleeves* (a short story collection), and a play, "Quintuples."

Mark L. Schneider is the senior policy advisor to the director of the Pan American Health Organization. Previously, he was on the senior legislative staff of Senator Edward Kennedy, and he served as Senator Kennedy's deputy issues director during the 1980 Kennedy for President campaign. He also served as senior deputy assistant secretary of state for human affairs from 1977 until 1979.

About the Editor

Pamela S. Falk is the associate director of the Institute of Latin American and Iberian Studies at Columbia University, where she is an adjunct associate professor. She was previously associate professor of international relations in the political science department at Hunter College of the City University of New York. She has also taught courses in the history of the Spanish Antilles in the Department of Puerto Rican Studies at the City College of New York. Articles by Dr. Falk have been published in the *New York Times,* the *Wall Street Journal,* the *Los Angeles Times,* and the *New York Times Book Review.* She is the editor of anthologies on Brazil and Mexico and the author of *Cuban Foreign Policy: Caribbean Tempest* (Lexington Books, 1986). Dr. Falk is a member of the Council on Foreign Relations and is on the board of directors of the Caribbean Cultural Center.